the Internet and Information Technology

Performance Measurement Made Easy

by

M. Victor Janulaitis
Positive Support Review, Inc.
Santa Monica, CA

First Printing September 1996

Published by:

Positive Support Review, Inc.
Santa Monica, CA

(310)453-6100
FAX (310) 453-6253
http://www.psrinc.com/psr.htm

Printed in the United States of America

HandiGuide is a registered trademark of Positive Support Review, Inc.

ISBN 1-881218-25-2

Table of Contents

Metrics HandiGuide® for the Internet and Information Technology

Performance Measurement Made Easy

by

M. Victor Janulaitis
Positive Support Review, Inc.
Santa Monica, CA

About The Author

 M. Victor Janulaitis has been an executive level management consultant since the late 1960's. His work in the Information Technology and Organization Theory arena is touted by many as some of the most progressive and forward thinking. He has helped many organizations to focus on the true value and costs associated with day to day operations that are dependent on computing power.

Mr. Janulaitis currently is the CEO of a very successful consulting practice based in Santa Monica, California. Clients he has served span many industries and are international in scope. His consulting is focused typically in larger enterprises going through periods of rapid change. In addition to his consulting, he has been called as an expert witness in trials associated with organizations that have downsized.

He was one of the developers of the ASAP system at American Hospital Supply that has been written up as a case study by the Harvard Business School. More recently he was the project manager for the roll out of the Infiniti, which also has been written up as a case study. His clients have included Merrill Lynch, AT&T, Kraft, Sizzler, Denny's, Avon, Hilton Hotels, Bank of America, Wells Fargo, Paramount Communications, and Time.

Mr. Janulaitis has developed a number of unique management methodologies that have helped many organizations to downsize, realize real profits, and improve customer service. He has been the keynote speaker at a number of international conferences, including one featuring Peter Drucker. He has also authored *"Client Server Management HandiGuide*®*," "Information Systems, Data Processing and Communications Metrics HandiGuide*®*," "Information Systems Position Description HandiGuide*®*," "PC Policies and Procedures HandiGuide*®*,"*and several others. In addition to the above he has taught and guest lectured at several major universities at the post graduate level - including the University of Southern California, UCLA, Harvard and IMD in Switzerland.

Acknowledgments

There are many people we would like to thank. We hope they understand that it is always difficult to identify every individual who gave us insight, inspiration and support.

My best friend and most supportive critic, Carol Janulaitis is one person that deserves the most thanks. Many other individuals have helped in the creation of this book. They have included the staff members of Positive Support Review and other professional colleagues. Two of these individuals are Robert Laskey and Victoria Isip. Special thanks to Michael Janulaitis who generated the network ready electronic version of this book.

In addition, over the years various colleagues at several organizations have contributed to our experiences and metrics. We have defined metrics and process to capture and present them to all levels of management for various industries including banking, entertainment, retail, financial services, government, distribution and manufacturing dealing with these specific issues. We have drawn heavily on that material and have sought to protect our clients' confidences. Any specific reference to any metric or approach is supported by several actual implementations of it in real life situations.

To all we give thanks.

Foreword

Metrics HandiGuide® for the Internet, and Information Technology

Introduction

Historical Perspective

Since the late 1960's, the working world has been inundated with computers and new technologies. Few people have understood them but everyone has needed them. Since the cost of this technology was and remains high, many attempts have been made to create meaningful measures and metrics. Most have failed in their primary objective -- to show the value and efficiencies of the application of these technologies in the enterprise. This has resulted in a total lack of consistent operational and performance measures.

Traditionalists have tried to measure the efficiency of computer equipment, communications equipment and the processing of data. Management has continued to ask how a percentage of utilization on a computer will impact customer service or the bottom line. Few measurement systems have explained that high utilization of a computer system can cause slow response time, thus adversely impacting customer service. Even with the many reporting systems in place today, most organizations, if they are lucky, know tomorrow how they did yesterday. Many don't even know that.

Imagine going to south Florida after a hurricane and seeing all the roofs that blew off. A comment that new building codes are required would be expected but is not adequate. That response did not help when the hurricane was there. The same is true for after the fact reporting of performance of computer systems. It is management by "rear view mirror".

What we have is a high cost operation with no generally accepted performance standards for its operation. In the manufacturing world that is like saying that we have a product that has high raw material and labor cost and we do not know on a day-to-day basis how efficiently and effectively the factory is running. Thus the need to measure and have valid metrics is an area of great focus.

The need to measure is based on management's requirement to understand the value received by technology. At the same time they need to balance the risks. Value can be in traditional financial or social returns of strategic parity between the enterprise and technology, or parity between the enterprise and its competitors through technology. This then is often balanced against risks the technology brings including risk of failures due to the technology implementation, operation or existence in light of enterprise strategic and tactical needs.

As with any mature industry and function, Information Technology, Information Systems, Communication and Data Processing (referred to as IT throughout this book) require metrics that are meaningful and manageable. In this book we present a view of measures and metrics that we have helped many organizations implement over the last several years. What is presented is a collection of measures that we have found to be the best. We have designed our metrics and reports[1] in a way that most non technologists can understand them -- graphically.

Metrics Book Structure

The book is divided into several major sections. The first few are an overview of the book and a management summary that can be used by the reader as a guide of what to measure and why. The next sections of the book are a detailed presentation of measures and reports that effectively communicate the value and effort associated with the IT function. The final section provides the reader with examples of the metrics and reports discussed throughout the book.

Organizational Responsibilities

Before any design, much less implementation, of metrics can be successful the organizational needs and responsibilities need to be well understood. In this section we will present one point of view of the organizational responsibilities that need to be defined before a successful process can proceed.

Internet, Electronic Communication, and LANs

As the use of IT has spread, so to has the use of workstation-based forms of information exchange. Such electronic communication may take the form of notes sent to and received from users (e-mail), notices posted to a central location for all users to read (bulletin boards), or software used jointly by each member of a work group to organize time and work projects (groupware). This section provides a brief overview of what this technology encompasses.

Metric Design

The real measure of any reporting package is how senior management and the customers of IT view its value. One of the first steps in providing the necessary value is to make sure

---

1   All of the reports presented in this book have been produced with Positive Support Review's IT Metrics Reporting System and UVP (User Vision of Performance) Monitor.

everything that is measured and reported ties IT to traditional business performance statistics and customer service metrics.

Presented in this section are metrics that we have classified into the following groups:

- ❐ Financial
- ❐ Staffing
- ❐ Internet - Electronic Infrastructure
- ❐ Competitive/Comparative
- ❐ Productivity
- ❐ System Development
- ❐ Reengineering - Office Automation[2]
- ❐ Quality Assurance
- ❐ Help Desk
- ❐ Computer Operations
- ❐ Communications
- ❐ Other - Technology
- ❐ Enterprise/Industry Specific

For each of these areas there is a discussion of metrics and how they can be measured. As you can appreciate, this cannot be an all inclusive list but it should be a definitive statement of what types of metrics can and should be used.

Metrics

This section of the book defines the metrics discussed in the management overview. The metrics are classified by category and report. Actual report examples are presented in the last chapter of the book. This section of the book can be used by the reader to structure his/her own monthly and annual reporting package.

Included is a discussion of data presentation techniques and rules to be followed that we have found to be the most effective with management and user groups. Suffice it to say that graphics are the most easily understood and misused tool in most organizations. Using the sample reports presented in this book the reader will be able to cut to the heart of the necessary metrics.

As a note of caution, we advise the reader to frequently re-evaluate the value of every metric used. One of the most common faults in

---

2   Since Reengineering and downsizing is so prevalent in industry we have included one set of reengineering metrics that we have help to implement in the area of office automation. These can be used as a model for other areas.

place in many reporting systems is continued gathering of unneeded information. Here is an example of one such case.

> *In the course of an operations improvement project we discovered a reporting department of 210 people in a large publicly traded corporation. In a review of the reports that department produced we quickly discovered that they were gathering and controlling information on some very specific operating results. The accuracy of their information was without question excellent. The problem was other reporting systems came up with the same information with nowhere near the overhead associated in obtaining the same information.*

> *Quickly we restructured how the information was collected. We are very proud that we were able to eliminate all but one employee out of the reporting department. A staff reduction of 209 people. The CEO of the company asked us why we had to retain the single individual. We told him it was in order to produce a particular report that he had requested to have for his monthly operations meeting.*

> *The CEO sat back and said that the information was not worth enough to justify the salary of a single employee.*

The bottom line is to always re-evaluate the cost of your reporting systems and metrics versus the benefit received.

Metric Implementation

This section of the book provides the reader with an implementation plan with key rules that should be followed to integrate metrics and Service Level Agreements (SLAs) into his or her enterprise.

One of the tenets that we continue to follow is that whatever we measure will change. Therefore we need to be able to implement new metrics and SLAs quickly and effectively. Another example of this is a company that grew from nothing to a multi-billion dollar enterprise in less than five years.

> *As the company started its growth, it was very capital intensive. All the efforts of management were focused on jumping into new markets as they opened and providing the necessary customer service to preclude competitors from investing in the same markets. Within seven years the industry was saturated and the company had to look at how to maximize the revenue that it was getting from its customers.*

As you can appreciate, the SLAs and metrics to measure the growth of the business evolved rapidly over a ten year period. The IT function had to adapt the service it was providing to its changing business. They implemented an excellent metrics program not just for IT but for the entire company based on the concepts discussed here.

It is interesting to note that the top information systems executive has remained with this company the entire time. Were the metrics the cause or the effect?

Data Capture

A discussion of a user's vision of performance is presented in this section. Included is a discussion of various types of tools that can be used to help accomplish this. Features and functions of how to measure service as perceived by the user are discussed in detail.

IT Metrics System

The IT Metrics System and how it can be modified is shown here. This can be used as a model for creation of a system to produce all the metrics and reports discussed in this book.

Sample Reports

This section of the book will provide actual examples of the reports. Each of the reports will be depicted as they actually print using Positive Support Review's Metrics HandiGuide® software.

Appendix

The appendix contains materials that will help the reader to better understand the materials covered in this book and the Information Technology (IT). Included are:

- ❐ Glossary of Terms
- ❐ Other PSR Offerings
- ❐ Index

Organizational Responsibilities

A common concern in many enterprise-wide operational management approaches is needed to maximize value, while protecting technological resources (including PCs and work-stations) and assuring their availability to support all enterprise functions. The purpose of this HandiGuide is to provide an enterprise with the tools to effectively and efficiently measure all of the capital and information resources associated with technology. This includes both the operations and development of applications in the enterprise.

All elements of the enterprise's management metric process should be structured to maximize the value of operational results achieved versus a statement of what is being done. This includes:

❐ Assessing the value of the resource;

❐ Understanding if the resource is being utilized cost effectively;

❐ Maintaining a balance between needs, wants and what is achievable; and

❐ Communicating a balanced report card on the way the technology is helping achieve the enterprise's strategic objectives.

Base Assumptions And Objectives

There are a number of base assumptions associated with the operational management of the technology environment which were used in the creation of this HandiGuide:

❐ Integrated management with the enterprise's business functions of all technology components including operational management is necessary. Each of these components must be considered from a total-system perspective (i.e., the cost effective use and protection of information must be considered from its origination to its final destruction, to include all processes affecting the information).

❐ Operational management of the IT resources requires extensive policies, responsibility assignment and procedures to provide the necessary operational framework and infrastructure.

❐ Operational management complies with the intent of prevailing legislation.

❐ Operational management requires documentation, justification, and administrative controls which are cost-effective, prudent and operationally efficient.

❐ Good operational management requires monitoring the implementation of selected metrics, controls and procedures. This includes the definition of the functions necessary to ensure compliance with stated.

Operational management guidelines, as presented in this book, should be considered as the minimum standard for all processing and supporting metrics activities.

Given these assumptions we have tried to achieve several very specific objectives in this HandiGuide. The first and foremost is to provide a tool with which readers can create their own specific metrics in the entire enterprise[3]. With that as a primary objective, the other objectives are:

❏ Provide a uniform set of rules and guidelines;

❏ Provide pragmatic rules to ensure that metrics created and/or handled by computer and manual systems is protected in relation to the risk of loss, inadvertent or deliberate disclosure, fraud, misappropriation, misuse, sabotage or espionage of enterprise assets;

❏ Provide a method to disseminate "institutional learning"[4] on the metric process and environment within an enterprise; and

❏ Ensure the integrity and accuracy of all enterprise information.

With the use of this material, based upon an active and continuous metric assessment program, an enterprise should be able to create a process where the following elements of enterprise management can be successfully integrated and implemented:

❏ Ability to understand the value and contribution of the processes impacting enterprise information resources;

❏ Ability to view new processes and estimate the potential contribution of new approaches as they become cost effective;

❏ Ability in the systems development review and testing procedures to ensure enterprise's operational and senior management objectives are met in all designs, implementations and operations;

❏ Ability to deny access to resources based upon a defined set of implementation "hurdles" that all new solutions must face; and

❏ A realistic and exercised metrics creation and reporting process.

---

3   Readers of this book can submit a letter on their company letter head to request the "inclusion in part or in entirety" of sections of this HandiGuide in company manuals. The primary requirements are the inclusion of M. Victor Janulaitis' copyright and the final document be for internal use only (i.e. not for resale).

4   This it the information that is known to members of an enterprise that is normal and necessary to conduct business within the enterprise on a day-to-day basis.

Management Process

It is impossible to define a single detailed organizational structure that can be followed by all enterprises as they manage in the IT environment. However, this section provides a prototype organization approach which we have found to work in many situations.

Executive Management

The executive management of every enterprise is responsible for setting the direction of the business. Given the impact and magnitude of the cost associated with all computerized processing of an enterprise's "books and records", executive management must set the tone and direction for all technology. One of the most common approaches utilized by many enterprises is to have this group assign the overall "architectural responsibility" for technology to one functional area. This area is typically the enterprise's centralized IT department[5] or one of the 'better' operating group's IT staff.

General Operations Management

Managers at all enterprise levels are responsible for the operation of their IT activities and must ensure that all reasonable actions are taken to guarantee this operation is effective, efficient and in the best interests of the organization.

Each manager has the general responsibility for the operation of IT as well as for security and safekeeping of all enterprise assets within his[6] areas of control.

---

5   We do not intend to discuss the pros and cons of centralized versus de-centralized versus distributed processing. Nor do we propose any one way is better than the other, rather for ease, we call the "function" the IT Department.

6   In writing this text the author has decided to use his versus his/hers when referring to an individual in the organization. This is not intended to be sexist rather a convenience to the author and reader as his/hers is rather cumbersome.

> **The day-to-day operation of all technology is assigned to the group that has the most impact on the use of the system. PC and client server operational management is typically assigned to line operations and the "host processor" to a single group such as a centralized or divisional IT group.**

Individual Managers And Staff Members

Each manager and staff member should be held accountable for the operation and security of his job and function-related IT applications and resources. Individual managers and staff members should be evaluated on their performance as measured against those objectives.

IT Resource Group

The resource group is the basis for architectural decisions and tool selection to support this environment. They set the actual standards and provide the basis for continuity between various IT applications and processing (if any). This group is often the "Centralized Information Systems" staff. They are required to be ready to select new tools and be the backbone of any implementation effort. The individuals in this group are typically information system professionals.

Support Staff

The support staff typically reports to the operational groups with a dotted line relationship to the Resource Group. This group is responsible for the day-to-day operations of the IT system. The individuals in this group are a mix of information systems professionals and operational staff. This group, in many successful organizations, is viewed as a training ground for future operations management staff. Additionally, within these same successful organizations over 50% of the individuals on these staffs are "seasoned" enterprise employees. They usually have at least seven to ten years of experience in the way the enterprise does business. They have the necessary institutional knowledge to help leverage this technology.

This group has the ability to make major enhancements to the systems without any help from the resource group. However, they do so based on the standards as defined by the resource group.

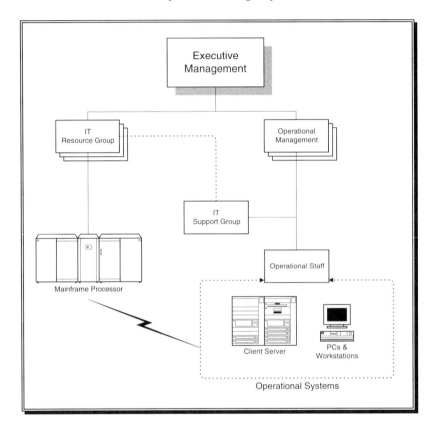

Figure 1 - Generic Organization Chart

Responsibilities

The embedding of computers into virtually every enterprise function and process dictates that IT operations cannot be viewed as a minor technical matter falling under the exclusive purview of the operations management community. To the contrary, the vital functions of the computers and the potential impact upon the enterprise of system shortcomings make IT (including PC, LAN and Work Station) operations a serious concern of all levels of enterprise management.

The objective of an enterprise IT management process is to achieve an effective and cost beneficial operating posture for the enterprise's IT environment. Attainment of this objective requires a balanced combination of problem recognition, resource allocation and policy focus to implement an effective program.

This section defines the responsibilities for all levels of the enterprise's management, support staffs, and committees in order to assure successful implementation of the enterprise metric management, control and oversight process. It also describes the activities required of other organizational entities in support of the enterprise IT management, control and oversight process[7].

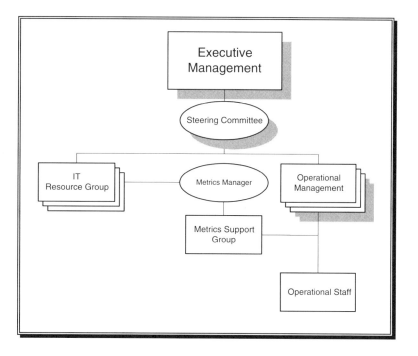

Figure 2 - Organizational Responsibilities

7   Refer to Information Systems Position Descriptions HandiGuide published by Positive Support Review, Inc.

Manager, IT Resource Group[8]

The manager of the IT Resource Group, often the enterprise's CIO, is responsible for the enterprise's IT oversight process and for ensuring compliance with management policies. In this capacity the manager should:

❑ Provide the resources for the development, implementation and maintenance of policies, plans and procedures to manage the overall enterprise IT process, infrastructure and metrics;

❑ Provide the identification and communication of IT related problems, new requirements and resource needs to the enterprise's executive management; and

❑ Represent the interest of the enterprise IT applications and systems to the enterprise's planning and budgetary review bodies. For many enterprises this is the Strategic Planning Committee.

Manager, Enterprise Operational Group

The manager of each operational group is responsible for the management of all IT operations in his area. In this capacity the manager should:

❑ Designate and provide staff necessary for developing, operating and maintaining IT resources, infrastructure and metrics for the activity; and

❑ Manage all of the resources dedicated to IT applications to ensure that they meet and support executive management's enterprise wide objectives.

Steering Committee

The Steering Committee is responsible for:

❑ Approving policy, standards, procedures and guidelines on all matters relating to the processing of

---

8   This individual is called many different thing is organizations. In the early 1990's, the title of CIO - Chief Information Officer was coined.

❒ customer, staff member and enterprise information. This includes all aspects of all applications of technology; and

❒ Overseeing the enterprise's IT metrics implementation and operation process. This includes establishing, funding and staffing projects as necessary for metrics activities, facilities, and other resources.

Manager, Metrics

The manager of the Metrics is responsible for overseeing the enterprise's metrics development, implementation, re-assessment and operational needs and requirements. In this capacity the manager should:

❒ Ensure the integrity of the enterprise metrics;

❒ Maintain a staff with current knowledge in metrics technology and the ability to determine its applicability to the enterprise's operations;

❒ Interface with all enterprise managers, directly or through their representatives, on matters that relate to or are unique to their areas;

❒ Develop operational control and security policies, standards, guidelines and procedures relative to the physical, personnel, data, communications, hardware, and software aspects of metrics;

❒ Review and approve the categorization of each metric;

❒ Review and approve specifications prior to contracting or programming applications and changes; and

❒ Maintain direct operational control metrics.

Enterprise Managers (Groups, Departments and Divisions)

All enterprise managers should be responsible for:

❒ Developing an understanding of the sensitivity and criticality of enterprise information and IT, as well as formulating basic statements of business objectives, requirements and specifications for their applications;

❏ Assisting the Metrics group in design, development, re-assessment and operation of systems that support the metrics process;

❏ Supporting, with technical assistance, any project where specific functional expertise or advice is needed; and

❏ Evaluating staff members on the nature of support rendered to the enterprise's management through performance evaluations, comments and/or ratings.

Enterprise Staff Members

Staff members are responsible for adhering to the enterprise IT management policies, standards, guidelines and procedures. They should also assist in the identification of metrics that have, or could, improve or inhibit the effective and efficient utilization of all IT resources.

Asset Owners

All computing resources should be assigned to an owner, however, this does not imply full rights of ownership (i.e., the enterprise retains the rights to authorize the sale, distribution or destruction of a resource). The owner is the senior executive responsible for the assets controlled by a system.

Asset owners are responsible for specifying the:

❏ Meaningful metrics;

❏ Level of quality expected;

❏ Rules associated with all data, information and calculations;

❏ Authorized use of the resource; and

❏ Access authority of each user.

Only the owner of a resource should have the authority to approve a change to the access control restrictions previously specified for that resource.

Owners of data are responsible for reviewing access to that data. Owners are also responsible for determining the following resource characteristics:

    ❑ Value, importance and specific business purpose; and

    ❑ Level of reporting that is required.

In the mainframe environment, the owners, as defined in the Responsibility Matrix that follows, are responsible for IT resources.

		Systems	Applications
Data	Production	Development Group	End Users
	Test	Software Engineering	Application Support Group
Software	Production	Development Group	Development Group
	Test	Software Engineering	Application Support Group
Commands	System Operation	Development Group	
	System Maintenance	Software Engineering	
Transactions	Production	Development Group	
	Test	Application Support Group	
Address Space (Capacity)		Development Group	
Documentation		Application Support Group	

Figure 3 - Responsibility Matrix

Support Managers

The Support manager is the manager responsible for the operating integrity of a system. This manager must be of vice president or general manager level or above. The individual is responsible for requesting appropriate establishment or modification of the access control restrictions for an IT resource. This request requires approval of the owner of that resource.

Users

Users of enterprise data, software and documentation are responsible for:

- ❏ Using these assets only when authorized and only for approved purposes;

- ❏ Complying with IT operating policies and procedures, as well as approved internal controls for resource, and asset protection requirements; and

- ❏ Ensuring that data, software and documentation in their custody are not accessed, copied or distributed to unauthorized users.

Help Desk

The Help Desk is the first line of support for all users of IT services. In the case of PC users, this function is often augmented by outside users. The primary responsibilities of the Help Desk is as the name implies:

- ❏ Answer questions as they arise on application, software and hardware;

- ❏ Diagnose problems and provide solutions in an expeditious manner; and

- ❏ "Center Post" problem tracking and solution implementation.

The chart that follows depicts a sample problem resolution process with the Help Desk assuming a key role.

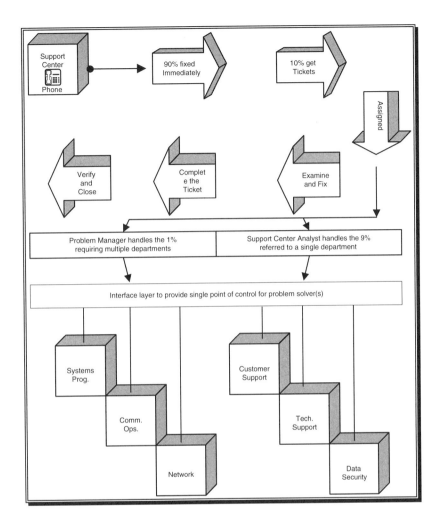

Figure 4 - Help Desk Problem Resolution Process

Outside IT Services

Outside IT services (this also includes the enterprise's own centralized IT department) are commonly used by many enterprises. Often they are managed by individuals with limited experience and knowledge of traditional IT and control concerns.

By providing specialized support utilizing contract resources over short or long periods of time, the enterprise can achieve both operating and financial efficiencies which would otherwise require long-term commitments or capital investments. Relationships with outside service personnel and organizations, however, present unique legal and operational situations which must be addressed cautiously in order to successfully fulfill an enterprise's objectives. Because of the sensitive nature of an enterprise's operations and the data it processes, effectiveness and security must be foremost considerations in the establishment and maintenance of these relationships.

Because those providing outside services may not have a high awareness or an appreciation for the requirements of the enterprise, the enterprise must address these needs which can be used to build a successful contractual relationship.

Operational management has the responsibility to ensure that outside IT services provided to the enterprise do not jeopardize the integrity of the enterprise's IT management, control and oversight processes.

Applicability

The following pertain to all contractual relationships, both contemplated and in force, for IT and data communications support and services.

The provisions outlined here are applicable to the operations and activities on behalf of the enterprise by centralized IT staffs, service bureaus and contract personnel, regardless of whether the service is provided on or off the enterprise's premises.

Responsibilities When Using IT Services

Managers, All Departments, IT and Support Groups

These managers[9] are responsible for ensuring that:

- ❏ All proposed contractors for support of their functional areas are capable of compliance with the provisions of this book;

- ❏ All proposed processing sites which could involve sensitive or critical enterprise data or processing are inspected by the Audit Department and approved by the IT Resource Group prior to commencing such activities;

- ❏ All proposed contracts for such service and support should be, at a minimum, reviewed and approved by the Contract Services Group and IT department[10];

- ❏ All proposed contractors understand their responsibilities for adhering to these policies; and

- ❏ All system identification numbers and passwords for use by contractor personnel are properly issued and withdrawn.

Managers, All Other Enterprise Departments

These managers are responsible for ensuring that:

- ❏ All proposed contracts which would involve automated processing of sensitive enterprise information or critical applications are, at a minimum, reviewed by the Contract Services Group and IT department;

- ❏ All proposed processing facilities which would involve sensitive enterprise data or critical processing are inspected by the Audit Department and approved

---

9   Detailed Job Descriptions for 200 positions in IT organizations are contained with the Information Position Descriptions HandiGuide published by Positive Support Review.

10   This applies if this is with a third party organization.

by the IT Resource Group prior to commencing such activities; and

☐ All proposed contractors understand their responsibilities for adhering to these policies.

Contract Personnel and Organizations

These contractors are obliged to support enterprise IT policies, standards, guidelines and procedures so as to meet those objectives. Contractors are responsible for ensuring that their staff members are fully cognizant of the importance of the IT application to the enterprise and their role in providing it.

Manager, Contract Services Group

This manager is responsible for ensuring that all enterprise IT contracts reflect the requirements outlined in this book.

IT Resource Group

The IT Resource Group is responsible for accomplishing on-site inspections of processing facilities proposed to be used for sensitive or critical enterprise data or processing. No outside IT processing area may be used for sensitive or critical enterprise information or processing without specific written approval from the IT Resource Group.

Manager, Audit Department

This manager is responsible for periodic on-site inspection of processing facilities which involve sensitive or critical enterprise information or processing.

Outside IT Services - Basic Policies

Outside IT service bureaus, organizations or agencies involved in providing support to the enterprise should be required to maintain a level of security commensurate with the sensitivity of the data being handled and the criticality of the IT and business functions supported. This requirement for security should be made a part of the contract and a condition of satisfactory contract performance[11].

Inspection

Before entering into any agreement for outside services which involve sensitive enterprise information or critical applications, an inspection of the proposed contractor's facilities should be conducted.

Security Regulations

Contract personnel should be bound by the same basic policies and procedures as pertain to the enterprise staff members. Contract IT personnel should be advised of the importance of the enterprise's IT and the conditions surrounding their engagement prior to execution of a contract for their services, and should be bound to protect the enterprise's assets.

Contract Performance Clause

Contracts for IT services should contain a performance clause regarding adherence to the enterprise IT operating procedures. This clause should stipulate that a violation of these procedures could be the basis for possible contract termination for cause.

Contract personnel should be authorized only for a degree of access to critical enterprise IT resources and sensitive information as is necessary for them to fulfill the terms of their contract.

---

11   Performance metrics should also be included in the contract.

Access to the enterprise computing resources from uncontrolled or non-enterprise controlled facilities must be approved by the IT Resource Group.

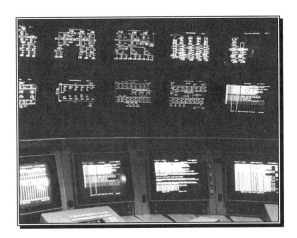

Internet, Electronic Communication, and LANs

As the use of IT has spread, so to has the use of workstation-based forms of information exchange. Such electronic communication may take the form of notes sent to and received from users (e-mail), notices posted to a central location for all users to read (bulletin boards), or software used jointly by each member of a work group to organize time and work projects (groupware). This communication may happen locally across the office LAN, across gateways to reach other company users and LANs at remote sites, or nationally or even internationally using dial-up services or the Internet.

There are many benefits to using electronic communication. It enables sharing of information without exchanging diskettes, as word processing and spreadsheet files can be attached to e-mail notes. It allows one message to be sent to many individuals simultaneously. Mailing lists of individuals can be made available so that anyone who needs to contact the members of a list may do so with one command. Corporate-wide information can be posted to an electronic bulletin board for all associates to read at their desks. Speed of communication is improved as well. E-mail messages are delivered quickly -- immediately across the LAN and within 1/2 hour over systems like the Internet.

Electronic Communication Usage Guidelines

The different types of electronic communication software serve various purposes. Below is a brief description of the major types of electronic communication vehicles. In the process of creating metrics all of the following areas need to be considered.

Electronic Mail

Electronic mail (or e-mail, as it is known) is used to send notes typed on the computer to one or more users who are connected in some manner to the user's system. The sender enters the note into the e-mail program, designating one or more addressees to receive it. On a LAN-based mail system the e-mail program forwards the note to the computer acting as the mail server. This is usually one of the primary file servers on the LAN. The mail server then checks to see if the addressee is currently logged onto the mail system. If so they are notified that they have mail. If not the mail server holds the note and delivers it when the addressee logs onto the mail system. After reading the note the addressee may either leave it in their mail folder, delete it, or archive the note for future reference.

Users should send items by e-mail that are intended only for one or two individuals or the members of a mailing list. For instance, e-mail might be used to send interoffice memos to selected individuals or groups. Or, by attaching a document from a word processing program, it might serve as a means of distributing drafts of a proposal to others for corrections and comments.

Users will generally be given an e-mail log-on when they are given access to the network. If they need a log-on but currently do not have one, have the user's supervisor submit a System Access Request on their behalf. Note that the user is requesting an e-mail log-on. Also have the supervisor add the new user's mail ID to any public mailing lists for the group or project.

To send mail to a public mailing list, display the Address Message dialog box. Double click on "Mail Lists" -- this will display all the available public mailing lists. To send mail to a personal mailing list, double click on "Private Mailing Lists" from the same Address Message dialog box.

Back-up and Deletion

E-mail messages require special handling. Regularly review mail that you have archived or that is sitting in a mail folder. Delete messages that are outdated or on which action has been completed. While it is true that messages left in mail folders[12] will be deleted automatically after 30 days, you should not rely on this fact to keep your folders tidy.

E-mail messages residing on mail servers are copied to back-up cartridges daily along with other file server data. E-mail is not as private as the U.S. Postal variety. Messages on mail servers or back-up cartridges may be examined in conjunction with certain legal proceedings. A word to the wise should be sufficient.

Appropriate Use

Messages sent via e-mail, bulletin boards, scheduling software, or any other groupware must be regarding company business only. Personal information may not be distributed in any of these ways, including any form of chain letter. In addition, the sending of any type of communication which is illegal (e.g. racial or sexual harassment) is prohibited.

The long-term storage of messages in network directories is also inappropriate. Message archiving must be done on a local hard disk or kept on a diskette. See the section above for more information on message management.

Bulletin Boards

An electronic bulletin board is an effective, unbiased method of communicating with a large audience. Someone posting a notice to a bulletin board would enter the information in the same way they would an e-mail note. The note is then forwarded to the bulletin board server (usually the mail server) where it is listed with all the other notices posted to that particular board. Users logged onto the mail system may (and should) then call up the boards they have access to and check for new postings.

---

12   This is based on parameters set by the "postmaster" in your enterprise.

Bulletin boards can become overcrowded with postings, causing important notices to be overlooked in the process. As a result, postings should be of general interest to the board's subject. They should not be made if e-mailing the information to a public mailing list, a private list, or individual mailboxes would be a more effective means of communication.

Maintenance

A bulletin board must have pertinent and useful information posted to it every month. Otherwise the need for the board will be re-evaluated and the board deleted if it is no longer required. Boards consistently used improperly may also be deleted. The IT administrator will notify board users and the local contact person when a particular board is to be deleted.

Internet

The origins of the Internet can be traced to a project at University locations attempting to test a system that would allow computers of various manufacturers to communicate with one another over the telephone rather than by magnetic tape or punch cards. The idea was to allow computers, manufactured by companies such as Burroughs, Digital, Honeywell and IBM, to "talk" to each other. The project was commissioned by the federal government's Defense Advanced Research Projects Agency (DARPA). Growing from early "e-mail" projects, the root of the Internet was officially launched in 1973 when the first networked computers communicated across multiple, linked packet networks. Initially, the agency's computer network consisted primarily of University locations. These initial attempts would evolve into what has been referred to in the media as "Cyberspace" or the "Information Highway," or what is officially known as the Internet.

Today, the Internet has evolved to a world wide network of computers that supports a variety of users. The growth of the Internet has been spectacular. Some have forecast a growth from approximately 30 million users in 1994 to 250 million by the year 2000. A recent study highlights that commercial sites now dominate the Internet (with approximately 50 percent), followed by educational, personal, government and other (such as trade associations). Having your own "Home Page" has become essential to most major firms and is catching on rapidly with medium and even small firms. A whole Internet industry has emerged to support this latest technology offering. In terms of accessing the Internet, "Surfing the Net" has become the latest entertainment option with consumers.

In today's environment it is now possible to communicate all around the world with an Internet connection. One of the unique things about the Internet is that it offers computing for everyone. Anybody can set up a rudimentary home page on the Internet at a relatively low cost.

In the office, businesses are groping with selecting the best method of supporting the Internet. As with all new technologies, the issues of security, potential employee abuse and privacy are foremost in most planning efforts. Many firms have taken the safe route by outsourcing the Internet to a third party provider (hence, outsourcing the issues). Business exposure is limited when an outsourced provider is used. Typically, business exposure is limited to e-mail or secured download/uploading of files. In those cases where a business has taken on the Internet directly, extreme caution must be exercised to minimize business risk. Below is a sample configuration linking several PCs with the Internet using an office network.

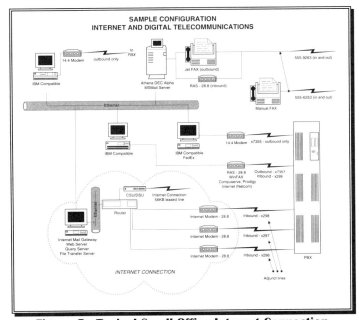

Figure 5 - Typical Small Office Internet Connection

Internet Characteristics

No discussion of the Internet would be complete without a brief description of its key characteristics. These are presented as a basis of understanding the discussion of security that follows. They are not intended to provide the reader with a comprehensive understanding of the Internet. For that we suggest that the reader obtain one of several books on the subject. In response to security concerns, may organizations have implemented private networks based on Internet protocols and conventions discussed below. These networks are often called "Intranets".

Electronic Mail (e-mail)

In the past, Electronic Mail (or e-mail) was the most popular Internet application. The Internet provides an inexpensive and relatively fast way to send electronic messages world wide. The cost of sending an e-mail message is generally included in the basic connection charge to the Internet. The globalization of e-mail along with widespread access by users will radically change the business of traditional paper mail providers such as the Post Office and express mail vendors. Today, Internet e-mail is somewhat restricted in size of message and capability to handle attachments such as files. Like most technology, this is likely to rapidly change. In the long term, traditional mail providers must either adapt or diversify to maintain their revenues.

File Transfer Protocol (FTP)

File Transfer Protocol, or FTP for short, is the main Internet technology for locating and downloading files from a server. The files can be anything whether it be text, graphics, audio or video. In its native form, FTP can be somewhat technical to use, but most browser software providers have made the user interfaces easy-to-use. The most important consideration in using FTP to download files to your business environment is the security risk associated with viruses. The file should be firewall protected (see Security topic below) and virus scanned prior to importing it into your production computing environment.

Gopher

A Gopher is a system of menus that can lead you to information that you want. Hence Gopher is short for "go-for" information. The problem with the Internet is the amount of information available exceeds the user's ability to find it. The use of Gophers has been developed to assist users in finding information quickly. *Archie* is one gopher program that typically was used on the Internet and still is available from a number of sources. However, it has been superseded by a number a generic general purpose search engines and "WEB spiders"[13].

Home Page

A rudimentary set up of a home page (also referred to as a WEB page) can be established quickly. More elaborate pages require considerable artistry and can incorporate pictures, high-tech graphics, audio and video. The viewer (user) must have suitable software installed on their PC to utilize the more sophisticated media offerings.

The reason that a home page is easy to construct is that it is really just text files that contain special hypertext codes (called HTML codes). These codes allow the user's PC (called a browser) to view the text in a Windows-like manner. The HTML codes allow for the software used by the browser PC to interpret the text and associated codes to display bold, italics, and jump via hypertext links to other files or pages. The HTML capabilities also provide for the insertion of graphics, audio and video. The HTML coding occurs at the beginning and the end of text lines to indicate new paragraphs, bold, italic and other text display attributes. For those familiar with early desktop publishing software (such as Ventura Publisher) or early mainframe products these codes are similar in nature to publishing tags used by those packages to allow display of bold, italic and centered text on a printed page.

---

13   A spider is a program that automatically searches WWW pages and develops electronic indexes based on what it finds.

TCP/IP Network Protocol

Transmission Control Protocol (TCP) and Internet Protocol (IP) was developed in 1974 by DARPA as part of the initial project efforts. Virtually all leading computer and software vendors now offer TCP/IP support. The network support offered by TCP/IP was adopted because it provides a means to communicate between mixed computer hardware vendor platforms. This network support is a practical and relatively reliable solution. It is also today's standard for getting Internet connectivity.

Telnet

The Telnet function allows users to access computer systems in a manner similar to traditional remote computing capabilities. In the Telnet use, the remote computer directly controls the program interface to the user's screen. Telnet systems are similar to signing on to a site such as CompuServe. Like signing on to an on-line service provider, most Telnet computers require log-on and password. In some environments, a guest log-on capability is provided. Today, they are primarily the domain of libraries, universities and government. Some businesses have also opted to use the Telnet approach to restrict access to a private circle of users. They typically use text based menus that lack the esthetics of the World Wide Web (WWW) browsers.

USENET Newsgroups

Newsgroups, the USENET, are public bulletin boards focusing on specific topics. Their initial focus was the Internet itself. Today, there are thousands of newsgroups on any and all topics of the day. Anyone is free to read the messages on the group and add their comments to the subject matter.

World Wide Web (WWW)

As popularity of the Internet has grown, so has its offerings. In addition to sending e-mail, Internet users can now avail themselves to sending files or log-on to remote computers for the sole purpose of obtaining new information about a product, service or an idea. The World Wide Web (WWW) is the user friendly portion of the Internet. Using special software to develop applications, the WWW site can offer Windows-like screens to the user. These screens have supplanted the traditional text based screens and menus offered in earlier on-line software applications. The WWW's foundation is based in client/server architectures offered today. In Internet terminology, the client is the "browser" and can be a PC, Macintosh or even a server (UNIX, NT or other platform). The "server" is the computer that contains the information to be accessed. Servers can contain e-mail, text files, databases and other types of files. TCP/IP is the communication protocol that allows the client to talk with the server.

The unique nature of the WWW is that the user does not need to know anything about the physical connection to the server supporting their browser. From a user's point-of-view, the connection is made by entering an address of the home page desired. The address typically might appear as "*http://www.psrinc.com/psr.htm*", which happens to be Positive Support Review's home page. The network provides the routing and mapping to the server location. The address to a particular site is known as its Uniform Resource Locator (or URL). A trip to Positive Support Review's home page will demonstrate how a typical business site can utilize WWW capabilities. In fact a number of readers of this book may have purchased it through the Internet. We have sold copies of other publications to WWW browsers in Africa, Asia and Europe. These are new customers from a new marketing channel.

Until recently, UNIX was the only available operating system choice as a WWW server. Today Windows NT, VMS and Macintosh are also being used as server platforms.

Security Concerns

The very essence of the Internet as it presently is deployed is built upon openness and easy access. These fundamental capabilities foster an environment where information can be easily compromised. While an inconvenience to personal users, in commercial situations, the results can be catastrophic. Security breaches of the net have been widely publicized. The fundamental problem presented by the Internet is its openness. The communication packets being routed on the net can be seen by anyone with the technical know-how to capture and interpret the information contained in the packet. The second problem presented by the Internet is intrusion by hackers. Hackers are technically adept users who seek to gain access to a server in a manner that goes beyond normal user access. Typically, a hacker is interested in gaining access to private files, causing damage in some manner, or they just want to see if they can beat the system. A more in-depth discussion of security is provided elsewhere in this book, but the fundamental means to address security on the Internet revolve around the following:

Firewalls

Firewalls are physical means deployed to isolate sections of the server environment. The purpose of a firewall is allow access to public areas of a server but to deny access to intruders to private sections of the server or to the businesses internal network in general. Firewalls can also be used to deny or restrict access to the Internet from internal users (to minimize potential employee abuse).

There are three basic methods of using firewalls to protect your Internet site. The protection is for invasion from the outside but also from internal wrongdoing. All three methods involve monitoring the addresses and ports specified in IP packets. IP packets have a header with a source and a destination address (as well as other fields). They are directed from a source to a destination by a router that reads the header information. Router screening is but one step in securing a private network. Even when the private network deploys a strong security strategy, in general, firewalls are but a first line of defense.

What is required in a security strategy? The starting point is aged passwords with rejection of easy-to-guess passwords, automatic log-out when inactive, and password replacement that prohibits easy-to-guess addendum's (for example, BOB1 replaced by BOB2). In other words, the traditional things that exist in today's non-Internet world.

Once a security strategy is chosen, there are many different ways of configuring an Internet firewall, the three basic ones are depicted below.

Screening Router

A screening router is the simplest type of firewall protection. Almost any router is capable of performing this function that evolves around accepting or rejecting IP packets based on the originating IP address and port as well as the destination IP address and port. Some routers have the capability to prevent "IP spoofing" as the packet enters the router. IP spoofing is a technique whereby the intruder attempts to fool the router into believing that the IP address and port are from a trusted inside host. Screening routers have a number of weaknesses, most routers for instance do not have the capability to log transactions (making it difficult to detect attacks). Some routers have more comprehensive logging capabilities that can even alert LAN administrators to a potential attack. Even in the best of logging circumstances, the capability of the screening router is no better than the rules programmed into it. Screening rules are generally applied in the order in which they are written. This makes writing screening rules far from a trivial task. A slight error in logic can open the private network to attack.

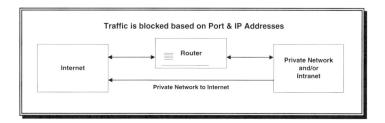

Figure 6 - Screening Router

The key to this technique is that the router is the focus of security. If the addresses are incorrect from either direction (upper line) the router inhibits communication. Both the port and IP addresses must be correct in order for the Internet to communicate with the private network. The private network can communicate with the Internet without security.

Dual-Homed Gateway

The dual-homed gateway offers better security than the screening router. It prevents any incoming traffic from crossing between the Internet and the private network. Care must be taken to screen incoming files for viruses before passing them to the private network.

In this model the PC in the middle acts as the gatekeeper. There is no direct link between the Internet and the private network as was the case with the screening router.

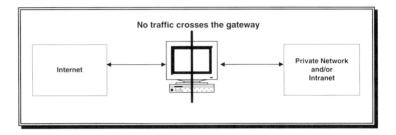

Figure 7 - Dual-Homed Gateway

Screening Router and Bastion Host

A still more comprehensive approach to the Internet firewall is the Bastion host and screening router approach. The Internet can only communicate to the private network via the Bastion Host. The private network can communicate through the host or the router.

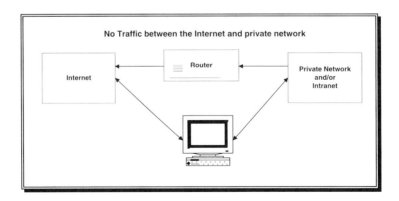

Figure 8 - Bastion Host

Firewalls are not a panacea. A poorly deployed one may be worse than none at all, since it may give rise to a false sense of security. On the other side if the site becomes too paranoid, all business function may be lost. This dilemma is one reason that many business sites have chosen to outsource until security issues are better resolved by the vendor community.

Encryption

Today, computer software is making extraordinary gains in providing low-cost encryption capabilities to a wide number of users. Encryption can be used to secure communications on the Internet. While effective in closed circle communications (communications to and from a know set of users) it is more difficult to deploy in mass audience situations.

The primary requirements for general business capabilities, such as the transmission of credit card information, on the Internet are still being addressed. In the case of credit card transactions, credit card providers such as Visa and MasterCard are developing solutions to the privacy/security issues related to using a credit card on the Internet.

A software package widely available on the Internet is PGP (Pretty Good Privacy). It can be used by non-commercial users to secure e-mail correspondence. Commercial products have been developed by several organizations who license commercial rights to use encryption technology in vendor software products. Vendors have made encryption capabilities more user friendly by integrating the core features directly within their products. At present, US laws prohibit the export of these encryption technologies to other countries. But since PGP is "freeware" and given the global nature of the Internet, its access has spread rapidly outside the US.

Netscape Communications Corp., the largest software provider for the Internet, has recently announced a Secure Courier capability within their product. This capability will let users create a secure digital envelope for financial data on the Internet. Since the product is new, it is not possible to render an opinion as to its effectiveness.

Policy and Procedures

Unless deployed with adequate policy and procedures, physical measures such as Encryption and Firewalls are ineffective. If e-mail messages are to be encrypted based upon discretion (verses automatic encryption of all messages), a tightly defined set of policy and procedures must be defined to clarify when and how a message must be encrypted.

The building block for developing policy and procedures is the development of a comprehensive Security Strategy and Plan. The plan should include all elements of protecting your Internet site against all risks. It should include passwords, firewall considerations and encryption, as well as other comprehensive security elements discussed elsewhere in this book.

Policy and procedure work must be detailed enough to communicate the rules of operation but not so cumbersome to deter reading of the rules. Positive Support Review has had a great deal of success in developing "Electronic Book" versions of Policy and Procedures. Our clients have found that electronic versions significantly add value to an overall security effort by allowing policy and procedures to be updated quickly and reviewed by an easy-access help file.

Pitfalls

There are least three areas where the best of organizations face serious pitfalls.

- ❏ Service Installation Delays
- ❏ Hardware Complexities and Incompatibilities
- ❏ Software Limitations and Incompatibilities

Service Installation

Phone company installation is often delayed and filled with a host of problems such as frame relay switching versus direct line connection, signal strength, and wiring to local telephone company offices, which many times are difficult to diagnose and often do not show up in the normal line testing.

Provider Service Activation (your connection to the Internet) may be delayed because the providers are over extended and do not have a staff that speaks "English" nor "communicates" well. As a matter of fact, a large number of service providers rely on phone company delays to cover many of their own shortcomings.

Domain name registration (what the world calls you on the Internet, i.e. *psrinc.com*) can take 3-6 weeks; make sure it is submitted to InterNIC as soon as possible. Your provider must do this for you and you do not normally know that this has not happened on time, until you try to turn on the system and you can not talk on the Internet. If you want a particular name you have to make sure that no one else has taken it.

After domain name registration is complete the domain name(s) still need to be added to the provider's domain name server; this can add days until your Internet site is accessible by others. One provider does this only once a week. In that case if you miss by a minute you may have to wait a week.

Hardware

The hardware link is controlled by a box (CSU/DSU) that many vendors do not want you to program. If you leave the vendor the capability to program it for you remotely, you have left the door wide open for someone to break into your system.

Not all CSU/DSU's are created equal - it is not unusual for an inexpensive "black box" CSU/DSU to have problems on phone lines with marginal signal strength.

The router (the firewall) should support at least 56kb, ISDN, T1 and have multiple dial-up port capability. If it does not and communication volume picks up, the enterprise will have "flushed" several thousand dollars down the drain. There is no trade-in value for anything - it is worse than a car. If an enterprise goes cheap and slow, it will end up spending more in the long run when it has to upgrade.

Servers (WWW, FTP, Mail, etc.) should be as fast as possible, with plenty of memory and disk space. At a minimum the enterprise should use at least a 90 MHz with 2 gigs of storage. Another consideration should be the operating system. DOS will not do and Windows is not worth the effort. That leaves NT, Windows 95 and UNIX.

Software

Internet software has bugs. There is more than enough "freeware" that has not been tested and is not fully supported. Professional software developers are just moving into this field.

WEB readers are not all the same - the standard answer from many vendors is that a solution will be provided in the next release that is always going to come out "next week". WWW pages and forms need to be designed carefully and tested with a variety of browsers. One particular syntax for forms worked with all of the browsers we tested, except with Mosaic on a UNIX/Motif system, where it caused a general protection fault on our server. Not all operating systems are supported by all products - NT for example may not be supported to the level of UNIX for a particular Internet client and server products.

Local Area Networks (LANs)

A Local Area Network (LAN) consists of a group of computers that can communicate with each other, share peripherals (such as hard disks and printers), and, if desired, access remote hosts (mini-computers, mainframes) or other networks. A LAN consists of one or more file servers, workstations, and peripherals. LAN users may share the same files (both data and program files), send messages directly between individual workstations, and protect files by means of an extensive security system.

Intranet

As Internet protocols and their general acceptance increase, many organizations are starting to implement LANs using the protocols of the Internet. They are placing these networks into private nodes called Intranets.

Features

❐ **Data Sharing** - Provides a convenient method for sharing data with other LAN users. When a PC is connected to a LAN, all information on it remains "private." Read, write, and other access privileges are controlled by the owner or supervisor. Files can be copied from the PC to a file server if they are to be accessed by several users. Additionally, files on the network server[14] are as easily retrieved as files residing on a local hard disk.

❏ **Application Sharing** - Application programs loaded on the file server are available to all authorized users. This applies to both enterprise applications and commercial software such as Lotus, Access, etc. These popular packages are published in special LAN versions and the appropriate multi-user licenses must be purchased before they can be installed.

❏ **Peripheral Sharing** - Permits users to take maximum advantage of limited computer hardware resources such as printers, fax boards, hard disk storage facilities, modems, mini-computers, mainframes, and other LANs.

❏ **Connectivity** - When connected to a LAN, the user can also access other computer systems, such as remote mini-computers, mainframes, and other LANs. Generally, this includes terminal emulation, printer emulation, and file transfer. This enables improved communications among users working on the network.

❏ **Security** - Provides extensive security features to safeguard network data and application program files from unauthorized users. Most PCs can be used by anyone having physical access to the equipment. However, access to a LAN requires that each user enter a user ID and a password which can be used to verify identity. This combination can also be used to define the files and programs the owner is able to access.

❏ **Back-up** - Data files on the server should be backed-up on a daily basis. In addition, the user should retrieve especially critical files and make personal back-ups on diskettes, to be stored locally. This process ensures the protection of files accessed by

---

14   A network server is a file server that is typically accessed by anyone on the network as opposed to a "file server" that is shared with a limited number of users.

multiple users. Recovery from data loss and corruption due to file-server hardware failures and other unanticipated disasters is maximized.

Physical Components

LAN are based on various topographies. Ethernet is the most common and Token Ring follows as a distant second. Unfortunately most Ethernet networks (BNC, 2,BaseT, 10BaseT and 100BaseT) have some inherent limitations. Capacity being the greatest and the cost to migrate from BNC to 100 Base T is very expensive. Token Ring is limited by market size and is significantly more expensive than Ethernet and extremely complex to implement. These factors, in turn, defer the implementation of new features and functions which are normally aimed at the greater market share - Ethernet. With that in mind, the main hardware and software components commonly found in a local area network system are as follows.

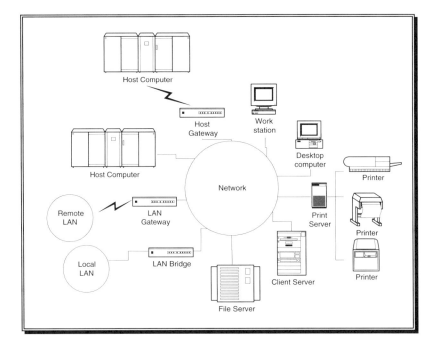

Figure 9 - Typical LAN Workstations

A stand-alone PC is known as a workstation after it is physically connected into the network and has accessed the network's operating system. When the workstation is configured with floppy- or hard-disk storage devices, the user may work independently of the network (locally). This PC configuration may have its own peripherals such as a printer, modem, or mouse. On the other hand, a diskless workstation has no disk storage devices and may only process programs and data files stored within the network system.

Network Cables

The computer cables facilitate the transfer of information between the different components of the computer system. Every workstation has several cables connected to ports (outlets) on the rear of the CPU. The network cable is the lifeline to the network resources, and should be protected from damage or detachment from the CPU. Some networks are wired in such a manner that, should a cable become damaged or disconnected, the entire network becomes disabled. If this happens, none of the workstations can process information over the network until the cable problem is corrected.

Network Adapters

Network adapters contain microchips designed to communicate with the network operating system. Without a network adapter, the computer would not be able to transmit, receive, or interpret any information processed on the network. Therefore, communication between network components would not be possible.

File Servers

The network cable runs from the workstation(s) to a centralized PC called a file server. The file server itself can be used as a workstation in some network systems, but it usually functions only as a central processing and storage point for network applications (word processors, database managers, spreadsheets, etc.) and data files. Shared peripherals, such as printers, are also connected to the file server. The file server has a hard disk, usually with a very large storage capacity. Network applications and network data files are stored on the file server hard disk, available for use by any user operating in the network.

Network Peripherals

Printers, modems, plotters, fax boards, and hard disks may be attached to the server, available for use by any workstation logged onto the network. When these peripherals are attached locally to a PC, the user may switch them between shared (on the network) and stand-alone (off the network) operation.

Network Operating System

Installed on the file server is the network operating system software that manages the network and electronically configures the file server so that the user can run network applications, manipulate network data files, and use networking features (i.e. peripheral sharing). It is a completely separate operating system from the normal operating system (e.g. DOS, NT, or Windows) and must be loaded into the PC before it will communicate (as a workstation) with the network server. The software is called the network shell and is loaded prior to accessing the network. The staff can provide you with the specific procedures for loading the network operating system into your PC.

Configuration

A typical LAN configuration is complex and has many variable components. There are a number of options available in the implementation of a LAN. The first deals with how the various PCs are physically connected. This is called the LAN topology. Some examples of this are token ring, star, network, and Ethernet. The second option is concerned with the driving software or network operating system. Some examples of this are NOVELL, Windows For Workgroups, Windows NT, and Lantastic to mention a few.

Users

Security considerations determine who may operate a workstation on the LAN. A single file server can store thousands of records and files concerning business data. The network operating system provides for different types of network users, each with their own network access privileges.

Network Supervisors

Network Supervisors are responsible for the efficient operation of the LAN. They maintain the network system, determine the security rights of any network user, provide guidance and training in the use of the network, create and maintain the primary directory structure for all the files and applications stored on the file server, and monitor the day-to-day activities on the network. Supervisors are also responsible for making daily back-up copies of the data stored on the file server in the event the file server crashes.

Regular Network Users

Any person who works at a workstation and has access to the network resources in the normal course of a workday is a regular network user. While on the network, these users may access any network feature that their security "rights" will allow.

Network Operators

A network operator is a regular network user who is given special responsibilities over certain network activities. These special privileges are assigned by the network supervisor. Network operators can provide valuable assistance to the network supervisor by maintaining some of the more routine network operations.

Security

To prevent entry into the LAN by unauthorized users, users will be assigned both a specific user name and a password by their supervisor. It is important to choose a password that would be difficult for someone else to figure out. If the password is written down, keep it in a safe place. A supervisor may have to change an individuals password periodically in order to keep a high level of security. When passwords are changed, a higher level of security consciousness is cultivated among workstation users, and overall security is improved.

Users should not give their password to anyone, nor allow other users to log-on with their ID's. If a user leaves the PC workstation for any length of time, they should log off the LAN so that passers-by cannot access the system.

LAN security can only be effective if the users maintain its integrity. It is the responsibility of each authorized user to keep the LAN secure.

LOGGING ON TO THE LAN

The supervisor can provide users with the appropriate start-up procedure for accessing the LAN. Also, the user will need to ask their supervisor for the following: the name of the network file server they are accessing, user name, and user password.

LOGGING OFF OF THE LAN

The user should be able to log off from any location in the network. It is important to properly exit any application that had been running on the workstation. The user must be certain to save the document so they don't lose any important data.

If there is a custom menu, select it to log off. Otherwise, type the appropriate log off command (i.e. LOG-OFF) and press the <<Enter>> key.

Directory Rights

The LAN security system is comprehensive and multi-layered, taking into consideration all the possible variations of user and organizational requirements for access to sensitive data. It also provides an extensive security system that can be used to restrict access to network directories and files. LAN users should not have access to every directory or file stored on the file server.

Users are assigned trustee rights. A trustee is any user who is given access to the directories and files stored on the network file server. Trustee rights are those security options that the supervisor assigns to the trustee.

In addition, the network supervisor can assign security restrictions to specific network directories and sub-directories. These restrictions are imposed by deleting a user's directory rights from the directory's "maximum rights" mask.

Directory and Trustee Rights	
Right	**Explanation**
Read from existing files (R)	The user can read the contents of a file that has no restrictions placed on it.
Write to existing files (W)	The user can edit the contents of a file that has not been restricted.
Open existing files (O)	The user can retrieve a file.
Create new files (C)	The user can create a new file. The user must have Write (W) rights in order to write data into the file and Open (O) and Read (R) rights to retrieve the file once it has been saved.
Delete existing files (D)	The user can delete files.
Parental (P)	The user can create, rename, and delete directories and sub-directories. The user can also assign access restrictions to limit use of directories by other users.
Search a directory (S)	The user can display a list of all files stored in a directory.
Modify file attributes (M)	The user can rename directories (if Parental (P) rights have been granted) and change the attributes of a file.

Figure 10 - Directory and Trustee Rights

When a directory is created, all directory rights are on the maximum rights mask and are automatically granted to the user. However, the supervisor can subsequently restrict a user's rights to work in a directory by deleting a directory right from the maximum rights mask. The exhibit 'Directory and Trustee Rights' outlines these security rights. The eight trustee rights and eight directory rights are the same, but each type of right is assigned separately.

A maximum rights mask exists specifically for each directory on the network, so the rights that apply to one directory do not apply to other directories. Changing the directory rights in one directory rights mask will not affect the rights in any other directory.

When a user is given trustee rights to a directory, those rights apply to succeeding sub-directories unless the supervisor assigns new trustee rights at a lower sub-directory level. In order to have access to a directory, the user must have both the trustee right and the directory right for that directory. This is known as having effective rights for a particular directory.

Home Directory

Because every company has specific needs and requirements, directory organizations are unique. The network supervisor will create a personal "home directory" for each network user. Your log-on procedure usually places you automatically in your home directory. It is in this personal directory that you will be assigned a maximum rights mask for your personal data files. This will allow you to read, write, open, create, and delete files within your directory. Other network users will not have access to your directory. It is here that you should store important personal data files and custom configuration files for application programs used on the network.

File Security

In addition to the comprehensive security measures discussed above, the network operating system also provides a file attribute security system to prevent an individual file from being edited by or shared with other network users. It is important to protect valuable files from being accidentally changed or deleted. Certain program files, such as DOS commands, are often restricted from being written in order to protect the integrity of the program.

Four basic file attributes affect the security of a network file. These security attributes are:

❐ **Read/Write** - Any user with the appropriate trustee rights can read from, write to, rename, or delete the file.

❑ **Read Only** - Any user with the appropriate trustee rights can read the file. The user cannot edit, rename, or delete the file.

❑ **Shareable** - These files may be read by more than one user at the same time. Large data files are often marked as Shareable.

❑ **Non-shareable** - These files may be accessed by only one user at a time.

When a file is initially created, it is marked as Read/Write and Non-shareable. Any user can edit, rename, or delete the file. The user will have to change the file attributes if the user wants to restrict access to the file after it is created.

It is important to note that file attributes take precedence over trustee and directory rights. A user may have full effective rights in a directory, but if a particular file has Non-shareable, Read Only attributes, that person cannot access the file.

Metric Process

Metric Design

Many organizations do not have a good mechanism for reporting on the value of the IT function. Typically, the reporting that exists is either of traditional financial accounting measures, that are bogged down in cost distribution, or detail technical data that shows the efficiency of the usage of the computer hardware. Neither of these approaches address the value added by IT.

A good metric and reporting process should meet the needs of several different audiences. This includes senior enterprise management, IT management, internal customers, and external customers. At the same time, it must help the enterprise achieve its business strategy while providing positive and negative feedback to the IT staff.

Figure 11 - Process Overview

In the course of developing a management reporting process for the IT function, these are three issues that need to be understood before idea one is put on paper. First and foremost is to understand what works well for one company, in one industry, may not work well for another company, in the same industry down the street. Corporate culture does play an important part in the process. Therefore, anything that we present here must be applied to an enterprise with its culture in mind.

The second issue is, once you measure, you modify behavior. If you measure the wrong thing or the right thing in the wrong way, the reporting system will become counterproductive.

The last and maybe the most important is that too much information is worse than no information. Probably the best case in point was highlighted several years ago in a large organization on the east coast.

> *The top IT executive in a large financial services organization had a total budget of $1.3 billion for technology. He had over 1,000 development and maintenance initiatives in process at any one time. If he received just a one inch binder per initiative each month, that would have been a stack of paper that was over ninety feet high. In that case he would have had too much information on too many activities and not enough meaningful information on the ones that were critical.*
>
> *A modified reporting process was put in place. First, a one page project status report was developed (See Project Status Report). Second, we put in place a filter, so that reporting would only include the initiatives that were over $250,000.*

This cut the number of pages down to 2 inches of one page project summary reports.

How many one page project reports for $250,000 projects have you seen?

As you design a Metrics Reporting package you deal with a number of complex issues. One of the first things that we do is to simplify the process; to identify specific user understandable metrics that we will measure, and to present the metrics in a clear and concise manner.

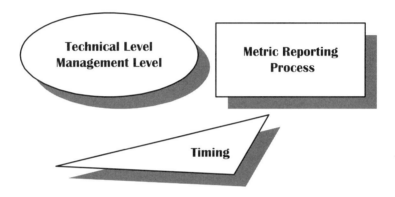

Figure 12 - Metric Issues Overview

Most organizations have developed reporting processes that do not take into account:

- ❐ Complex nature of the information
- ❐ Diverse needs and capabilities of the audience
- ❐ Diverse understanding of the audience
- ❐ Availability of metrics data and the metrics time windows

As you go through this book, we would ask you to remember that ours is only one view. This book will be a success for you if you can get only a few new ideas and implement them.

Reporting Audiences

As we look at the audience for metrics, we begin to understand the complex requirements they develop:

1. Organization
   - ❏ Internal IT
   - ❏ Internal Non-IT
   - ❏ External Customer
   - ❏ External Vendor

2. Management Level
   - ❏ Senior and Executive Management
   - ❏ Operational Management
   - ❏ Working Staff

The first step in the process of developing a metrics reporting system for your enterprise is knowing your audience. A second step is to understand the purpose of the metrics. Remember to measure is to modify behavior. Metrics reporting for the IT staff will provide them with feedback on their efficiency and effectiveness; for IT Management, it will provide a view of how well they are running the information factory; for the enterprise's management, the value of the IT function; for customers, both internal and external, objective measures of the service they are receiving.

Figure 13 - Metric System Audiences

Each of these in turn has an impact on the business strategy and how well the enterprise is working towards meeting its objectives.

There are so many interactions that occur in the course of day to day work. Metrics reporting must be viewed in the light of what will be accomplished once a report is produced and distributed in the normal operating environment. If a report is meant for informational purposes **_only_** -- that is, the readers are not going to modify their own behavior or do anything as a direct response to the report -- why send it? Most executives have too much to do and any excess information is a burden. For example, if two of the same information reports are provided to a marketing executive and an IT executive and neither does anything because of it, why send it?

That is not to say that informational reports should not be sent. What we are saying is to limit their audience. Many people and organizations have their own internal junk mailing lists that continue to operate past their useful lives.

> *In the review of an accounting process we asked one administrative manager what the most important report was that he had produced. This manager described a report that was produced weekly and was distributed to twenty-seven regional offices. The report tool required one case of computer paper or two reams of letter sized paper for the laser version of the report for each office.*

> *When we went to the regional offices we asked the people what they thought of the report and how they used it. One individual said that each week when the new report came in they took the old copy out of the file cabinet, shredded the report and put the new copy in the file cabinet. That was the only time the report was ever touched.*

There are many examples like this one that demonstrate how informational reports can be eliminated.

Reporting Levels

The same report the Chief Financial Officer finds as interesting and informative is typically not the same one that the lead Accounts Payable clerk uses to improve the day-to-day office operating environment. Even though they both converge in the same reporting organization, both of these individuals have different needs and interests. As the reader develops the metrics for the IT function this factor should be kept in mind.

The more senior an individual is in an enterprise the broader the scope of information required and the less depth. That is unless there is a problem. In that case, it is not unusual for senior executives to require much more detail. In any case, metrics reporting will need to keep this in mind.

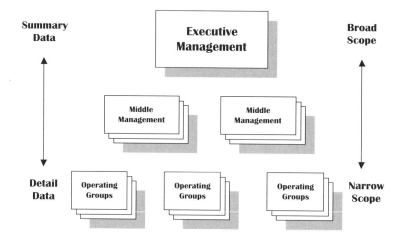

Figure 14 - Reporting Levels

One concept that you will see repeated throughout this book is a single page report. We firmly believe if an idea cannot be presented on a single page it is too complex to be meaningfully explained. More time should be spent to restructure its presentation.

This is a very important concept. If reporting is defined well, all levels will know when there is something they should be doing. They will be able to see that the proper impact is being made.

Report Groupings

We have developed a series of matrices that help in identifying not only the metrics to be used but also the types of reports to be provided to various individuals. In this part of the book we briefly describe each of the reports, the metrics reported, the people that could get the report, and the timing of the charts on the report. In the last chapter of the book *(see Sample Reports)* copies of the actual metrics reports are displayed. In addition to this, Positive Support Review's Metrics

HandiGuide® software produces each of these reports *(see Metrics System)*.

In the tables that follow we define the reports, groups and metrics that can be produced. On the top of the table are the names of the groups that will get the metric reports. On the side is the report that will be produced. The third dimension is the metric and timing of the report. This is a living matrix and one that has to constantly be revisited.

The IT reporting package documented herein consists of approximately 50 reports and 150 metrics. These reports cover IT's financial, staffing, and operational performance. They cover reporting required under Service Level Agreements (SLA) where appropriate. They also include information on project backlogs and status of the major active projects.

The individual reports in the IT reporting are designed for multiple audiences. There are four primary groups that we have defined within the enterprise. These are based on the management levels and organizational structure that we discussed briefly above. They are:

❐ **Senior Management** --
Chief Information Officer and his/her staff.

❐ **IT Operating Group Management** -- IT Management for overall performance and service level for major IT functions and, to report the significant details supporting the total, highlighting trends in critical measures.

❐ **Enterprise Senior Management** -- To report overall performance and service level for IT's total operation.

❐ **Customer Operating Group Management** -- Market Management to report IT's performance and service level for each market or business unit in accordance with the SLA contracts.

Report Types

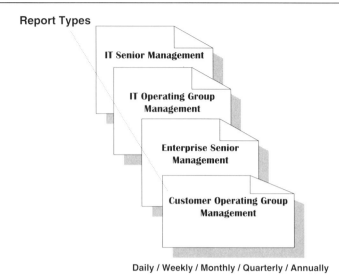

Daily / Weekly / Monthly / Quarterly / Annually

Figure 15 - Report Types

The categories of reports are:

- ❐ Financial
- ❐ Staffing
- ❐ Competitive/Comparative
- ❐ Productivity
- ❐ System Development
- ❐ Reengineering - Office Automation
- ❐ Quality Assurance
- ❐ Help Desk
- ❐ Computer Operations
- ❐ Internet - Electronic Infrastructure
- ❐ Communications
- ❐ Other - Technology
- ❐ Enterprise/Industry Specific

In the tables that follow we identify the individuals and groups that we "feel" should receive individual reports. The reader is advised that this is not gospel. Judgment should be used as to the reports to be produced, the frequency of each, and the breadth and depth of their distribution. In the last section of this book, most of the metrics that are identified here are presented in the form of sample reports.

Financial

The financial reports are typically reported on a month-to- month basis. For sake of presentation we prefer to show thirteen months. In this way, the metric report provides traditional year-to-date information and comparison of the same month this year and last year.

	IT Senior Management	IT Operating Group Management	Enterprise Senior Management	Enterprise Operating Group Management
Key Measures Report	Yes	Yes	Yes	Yes
Expense Summary	Yes	Groups	Part Year	Optional
Expense Variance by Category	Yes	Groups	Part Year	Optional
Expense Variance by Cost Center	Yes	Groups	Part Year	Optional
Capital Plan Performance	Yes	Groups	Yes	Optional
Project Capital Expenditures	Yes	Groups	Optional	Yes
Billing Allocation	Yes	Groups	Yes	Yes
System Usage by Customer	Yes	Groups	Yes	Optional
Resource Usage by Customer	Yes	Groups	Optional	Optional

Staffing

Staffing is an issue that is very dependent on the culture of the organization. Based on the organizational culture this may or may not fall within the IT Groups. For this reason, we have two versions of this matrix, one for centralized groups and one for distributed groups. Please note the same applies for a number of the functions that are in every enterprise.

Centralized

	IT Senior Management	IT Operating Group Management	Enterprise Senior Management	Enterprise Operating Group Management
Staff Plan Performance	Yes	Groups	Optional	Optional
Head Count Summary	Yes	Groups	Optional	Optional
Staff Turnover Report	Yes	Groups	HR	Optional
Protected Classes Summary	Yes	Groups	HR[15]	Optional

Distributed

	IT Senior Management	IT Operating Group Management	Enterprise Senior Management	Enterprise Operating Group Management
Staff Plan Performance	Groups	Groups	HR	Groups
Head Count Summary	Groups	Groups	HR	Groups
Staff Turnover Report	Groups	Groups	HR	Groups
Protected Classes Summary	Yes	Yes	HR	

In this distributed model, the staffing would be controlled and reported in the metrics system by whatever function has organizational accountability.

---

15   HR - Human Resources

Internet - Electronic Infrastructure [16]

Internet and World Wide Web activity is one of the areas where activity has continued to increase without regard to economic conditions and international borders. This is one area where a continued re-examination of metrics is a must.

	IT Senior Management	IT Operating Group Management	Enterprise Senior Management	Enterprise Operating Group Management
User Penetration	Yes	Groups	Yes	
E-Mail Traffic	Yes	Groups	Yes	
USENET Traffic	Yes	Groups	Yes	Yes
WEB Site Statistics	Yes	Groups	Yes	Yes
Electronic Commerce Volume	Yes	Groups	Yes	Optional
Volume Users	Yes	Groups	Yes	Optional

Technology will constantly change and its success is often dependent on the how extensively it is utilized by the enterprise. It is for this reason that we have found the "Volume Users" as one of the better metrics than can be implemented. With it you can identify the individuals and functions that are using the technology.

> *For example, in one organization the CEO personally calls each individual who has not used the new "electronic infrastructure" in the past week to "make sure that everything is working okay". Needless to say this encourages many borderline users into making sure they are not called.*

---

16   This can be the Internet, an Intranet, Notes or other such vehicle.

Competitive/Comparative

Competitive reporting is an area where great care must be taken to obtain information through ethical means. It is nice to know about one's competition, but it is important to see that comparative information is obtained only through legal means. Normally industry associations or industry publications can help in this.

	IT Senior Management	IT Operating Group Management	Enterprise Senior Management	Enterprise Operating Group Management
Revenue & Capital	Yes	Optional	Optional	Optional
Expenses & Staffing	Yes	Optional	Optional	Optional
Competitive Application Matrix	Yes	Yes	Yes	Optional
Technology Penetration Trends	Yes	Optional	Yes	Optional

This information is very important and should be kept up to date. It is extremely helpful to have this information when a merger or takeover is taking place or when someone in the enterprise asks the question about why a particular technology is being used in an enterprise.

Productivity

Productivity is probably one of the most difficult areas to measure in traditional IT organizations. Many of the best measures are those that relate to direct units of work or value. For example, the number of changes that have been implemented is a good measure since the customers have the best input into its measurement. Lines of code are typically a poor unit of measure for productivity.

	IT Senior Management	IT Operating Group Management	Enterprise Senior Management	Enterprise Operating Group Management
Development Productivity	Yes	Groups	Optional	
Production Support Productivity	Yes	Groups	Optional	
Response Time Reports[17]	Yes	Groups	Optional	Groups

This is one area where much work still has to be done with the movement away from centralized processors to object oriented and networked workstations.

It is important to define a unit of work that relates to the business terms. For example, in the airline industry a traditional measure is "Revenue Passenger Mile". A measure of productivity in that industry could be system development maintenance cost per revenue passenger mile. In the case of a manufacturing firm, system development maintenance cost per thousand units of "widgets" produced.

> *One drill bit manufacturer in the oil industry has all IT and communication expenses related to the per drill bit cost. When this measure was first put in, management of the firm had its eyes opened to the value added by this function. In addition to this, they then obtained comparative competitive data and used this to not only measure productivity but to help them make decisions on where they should apply their technology dollars.*

---

17   User Vision of Performance Reports

System Development

System development is not often in the realm of the user. In order to have good metrics, both the systems under the development control of the user and outsourcing vendors need to be included in these statistics.

	IT Senior Management	IT Group Management	Enterprise Senior Management	Enterprise Operating Group Management
Service Request Backlog	Yes	Yes	Yes	Groups
Project Status Report	Yes	Yes	Key projects	Groups
Service Request Aging	Yes	Yes	Yes	Yes
Service Request Closure Priority 1	Yes	Yes	Yes	Optional
Service Request Closure Priority 2 and 3	Yes	Yes	Optional	Optional
Conversion Status	Yes	Yes	Yes	Optional

As new systems are implemented in the networked arena they will have to be added to this set of metrics. If they are not, there will be a large gap in the quality of information that will be available to senior management in their strategic planning process.

Reengineering - Office Automation

Office automation can include all administrative functions for word processing, voice mail, and Local Area Network Applications that are geared to the administrative support staff.

	IT Senior Management	IT Operating Group Management	Enterprise Senior Management	Enterprise Operating Group Management
Reengineered Service Performance	Yes	Yes	Optional	Optional
Home Office Workers	Yes	Yes	Yes	Yes
Home Office Productivity	Yes	Yes	Yes	Yes
E-mail Usage	Yes	Yes	Yes	Optional
Voice Mail Usage	Yes	Yes	Yes	Optional
Project Status	Yes	Yes	Optional	Optional

Implementation of an automated voice response unit that links IT and voice communications could fall under this section or development reporting. Placing it in either is acceptable, but it should be done consistently for a single enterprise.

Quality Assurance

With the advent of programs driven by the Baldridge Award, much emphasis is placed on the quality assurance function.

	IT Senior Management	IT Operating Group Management	Enterprise Senior Management	Enterprise Operating Group Management
Test Results by Release	Yes	Groups		Yes
Release Test Comparison	Yes	Groups		Optional
Customer Satisfaction	Yes	Groups	Yes	Yes
Quality Improvement Program	Yes	Groups	Yes	Optional

The Test Results by Release is probably the first example of management of a system by something other than a feeling that a system is good. This concept has been applied by many successful development organizations.

> *A distributor of expensive foreign cars was in the process of creating a dealership for a new line of cars. In the process of that activity, they had over 500 people in the systems organization in their enterprise and 500 people in the systems organization of three other vendors working on this system. The Test Results by Release report was produced on a daily basis. The CIO and CEO of the enterprise said they would not have been able to deliver a quality system on time without that report.*

Help Desk

We have used the arbitrary term of Help Desk as the focal point for communication between technologists and users. In many organizations this responsibility is split between several organizations. In this case, we feel that at the very least, summary information at this level should be captured in a minimum of one place within an enterprise.

	IT Senior Management	IT Operating Group Management	Enterprise Senior Management	Enterprise Operating Group Management
Work Load Summary	Yes	Optional	Optional	Optional
Quick Incidents	Yes	Optional		
Problem Notification Analysis	Yes	Optional	Yes	
Problem Notification by Priority	Yes	Groups		Optional
Problem Notification by Category	Yes	Groups		Optional
Problem Closure Statistics	Yes	Optional	Yes	Optional
Installation Repair Management	Yes	Optional	Optional	Optional

Many organizations have this function in the user community. This must be taken into account in metrics measurement.

Computer Operations

This is probably the most difficult area to get good information. In many enterprises the single host computer system no longer exists.

	IT Senior Management	IT Operating Group Management	Enterprise Senior Management	Enterprise Operating Group Management
Computer Capacity	Yes	Groups	Yes	Optional
Combined Computer Work Load	Yes	Groups	Yes	Optional
On-Line Performance Summary[18]	Yes	Groups	Yes	Yes
E-Mail and EDI Traffic	Yes	Yes	Yes	Optional
Computer Outages	Yes	Groups	Optional	Yes
Batch Processing Performance	Yes	Groups	Optional	Optional
Billing & Report Distribution Performance	Yes	Groups	Optional	Yes
Charge Back Details	Yes	Optional	Yes	Optional

Communications

Communications include both voice and data communications. This is one area where many enterprises focus. With the advent of voice mail and other similar tools, usage and performance data should be consolidated for both of them.

	IT Senior Management	IT Operating Group Management	Enterprise Senior Management	Enterprise Operating Group Management
Network Outages	Yes	Groups	Optional	Yes
Electronic Commerce	Yes	Yes	Yes	Optional
Switch Performance Statistics	Yes	Groups		Groups
Voice Mail Performance	Yes	Groups	Yes	Groups

---

18   Refer also to the implementation section on the discussion of the User's Vision of Performance.

Other - Technology

This category is intended to be the base for new technology metrics. This is one area where metrics will continue to evolve.

	IT Senior Management	IT Operating Group Management	Enterprise Senior Management	Enterprise Operating Group Management
Workstations Analysis	Yes	Optional	Yes	Optional
LAN Analysis	Yes	Optional	Yes	Optional
Usage Analysis	Yes	Optional	Yes	Optional

Enterprise/Industry Specific

In the next section of this book there are a number of examples for enterprise/industry specific metrics. This is not an all inclusive list but some of the industries for which we have developed business operational metrics are:

- ❏ Distribution
- ❏ Education
- ❏ Entertainment
- ❏ Financial Service
- ❏ Government
- ❏ Hospitality
- ❏ Insurance
- ❏ Manufacturing
- ❏ Medical
- ❏ Real Estate
- ❏ Retail

There are other measures[19]. The ones we present, along with any developed within your enterprise, should be reviewed and maintained only if they provide value and assist the enterprise in operating more efficiently and effectively.

---

19   In the course of our consulting work we have developed many more metrics than are presented here. They are not included because in some cases the metrics are proprietary to the organizations that we developed them or in others they are too specific to an organization or management approach to have general applicability.

Metrics

One of the givens of the world of metrics is the fact that once you measure and report something you modify the results and behavior of the items and people being measured. Given this preamble, we have found that there are 11 areas where metrics matter in the IT world. The areas are:

- ❑ Financial
- ❑ Staffing[20]
- ❑ Competitive/Comparative
- ❑ Productivity
- ❑ System Development

---

20   This set of reports will vary more than most of the others presented based on the organizational structure used by the enterprise.

- ❏ Reengineering - Office Automation
- ❏ Quality Assurance
- ❏ Help Desk
- ❏ Computer Operations
- ❏ Internet - Electronic Infrastructure
- ❏ Communications
- ❏ Other - Technology
- ❏ Enterprise/Industry Specific

The reports are intended to be grouped in packages for the recipients. In addition, all of the reports are not produced each time period.

For example, while the financial reports are of great interest to many in the enterprise, there is no need for everyone to get every report. The marketing department does not have a need to get a copy of the Expense Variance for the Accounting Department. In addition, some of the reports the marketing department gets are meaningful daily (On-Line Performance Summary) while others are meaningful on a quarterly basis (Staff Turnover Report).

With this in mind, review the list of reports that are defined in the table that follows before proceeding to the individual metrics and format presented in each report.

As we progress, we will define a series of rules that should be followed in the creation of your metrics systems. What follows is a table of contents for the metrics of a 2.3 billion dollar corporation. This can be used as a guide for the level of metric reporting that your enterprise may want to implement.

In the report samples section that follow, most of the report templates for this sample metrics package are presented.

Report Categories

Category	Report Name
Financial	Key Measures Report Expense Performance Summary Expense Variance by Category Expense Variance by Cost Center Capital Plan Performance Project Capital Expenditures Billing Allocation System Usage by Customer Resource Usage by Customer
Staffing	Staff Plan Performance Head Count Summary Staff Turnover Report Protected Classes Summary
Internet Electronic Infrastructure	User Penetration E-Mail Traffic USENET Traffic WEB Site Statistics Electronic Commerce Volume High/Low Volume Users
Competitive/ Comparative	Revenue & Capital Expenses & Staffing Competitive Application Matrix Technology Penetration Trends
Productivity	Development Productivity Production Support Productivity Response Time Reports
System Development	Service Request Backlog Project Status Report Service Request Aging Service Request Closure Priority 1 Service Request Closure Priority 2 and 3 Conversion Status
Reengineering - Office Automation	Reengineered Service Performance Home Office Workers Home Office Productivity E-Mail Usage Voice Mail Usage Project Status Report
Quality Assurance	Test Results by Release Release Test Comparison (Special) Customer Satisfaction Quality Improvement Program

Figure 16 - Report Categories - Part 1 of 2

Category	Report Name
Help Desk	Work Load Summary
	Quick Incidents
	Problem Notification Analysis
	Problem Notification by Priority
	Problem Notification by Category
	Problem Closure Statistics
	Installation Repair Management
Computer Operations	Computer Capacity
	Combined Computer Work Load
	On-Line Performance Summary
	E-Mail and EDI Traffic
	Computer Outages
	Batch Processing Performance
	Billing & Report Distribution Performance
	Charge Back Details
Communications	Network Outages
	Electronic Commerce
	Switch Performance Statistics
	Voice Mail Performance
Other - Technology	Workstation Analysis
	LAN Analysis
	PC Usage Analysis
Enterprise/Industry Specific	Distribution
	Education
	Entertainment
	Financial Service
	Government
	Hospitality
	Insurance
	Manufacturing
	Medical
	Real Estate
	Retail

Figure 17 - Report Categories - Part 2 of 2

Graphic Data Presentation

Until recently, it was very difficult to present data in other than tabular form without a great deal of expense. The advent of PC-based graphics and laser printers have minimized that. Now artistic capabilities are available to everyone. The only limitation is one's imagination and artistic taste. Tastes and styles are now issues that creators of graphic reports must deal with.

Another problem that we now have is graphics that do not convey the ideas the data represents. As a guideline, definitions[21] have been made of good and poor graphic presentations.

Graphic Presentation Guidelines	
Good	**Poor**
Words spelled out	Abbreviations -- Acronyms
Legends and words on a single line	No legends and / or words that run over a single line
Discussion area to explain	Graphic that has no legend or a cryptic one
Shading that is well defined	Unclear coding with minor differences requiring repeated references to legend
Graphic that is pleasant and attracts reader	Graphic that is "ugly" and too cluttered
If color is used it is soft-blue	Multiple colors not taking into account "good taste", color implications, and color sensitivity (color blindness of reader)
Type is clear and does not overpower the graphic	Type is "loud" and overbearing
Upper and lower case type	Type is upper case and all bold

Figure 18 - Graphic Guidelines

---

21   Edward R. Tufte, The Visual Display of Quantitative Information, Graphic Press - Cheshire, Connecticut, March 1992

Data Presentation Rules

Many reporting systems have been developed in concert with traditional accounting data analysis and presentation. This has led to a certain amount of excess measurement of minute details that do not matter. As reports are produced out of computer systems, totals are traditionally printed on the last page. The best data is normally so buried that action that could be taken is taken too late or is not taken at all.

Rule 1	List summary totals on the first page of a report, not the last

Added to this accounting thrust, is the desire by many on the technical side of the IT business to be accepted by management causing too much irrelevant data to be captured and reported. We can all remember the reports that were produced by well intentioned individuals that provided no value except to the pulp mills that produced the paper.

Rule 2	Produce summary reports as the primary source of information

One Page Report

Most executives and managers do not have enough time to get their day-to-day functions completed in a cost effective manner. In addition, so much data crosses each individual's desk that summary data is the most beneficial. We have found the most powerful presentations of data are those that are the simplest and most easily comprehended. Once an idea crosses into multiple pages, many factors begin to take hold.

Rule 3	Produce One Page Reports

In the case of senior executives, we have found there are many who do not want to know the details of an issue. Rather they want to know what they need to know. It is more important to communicate back to them with the facts on the status of solutions and trends. They do not want to be the ones who find problems by reviewing data. That is the job of the individuals who are producing the reports.

One CEO told me that he spent his entire career hiring people better than him. He did not want to do their jobs for them. Rather he wanted them to do their jobs and give him the tools necessary to measure their performance.

Data Content and Timing

Most reporting systems in place are like the engineer who is measuring the size of the hole in the side of the ship as it is sinking. It would have been much better if time had been spent on a good radar system to show what was about to happen before it did.

Rule 4	**Design metrics that show trends not reports that show history**

In the course of a day or a week, so much information crosses the desks of decision makers that much of it gets lost. The only time that some of this critical information can be seen is when it is recast in a period reporting process. The key is to have a period reporting process that is responsive enough to allow for an enterprise to alter course.

Rule 5	**Have a formal reporting process that will drive decisions to be made before the report is produced and distributed**

Graphic Presentations

Data that is presented crisply and cleanly is much more valuable than a statistical table. USA Today showed the publishing industry the power of graphics. While that has been going on, the move away from computer screens that could just show characters and numbers to objects with sound and motion has accelerated.

Rule 6	**Use graphical presentations of data -- the graphic should do some of the analysis**

Analysis of data with graphic reports can simplify the communication process. If the data is presented as just a trend of a single item, then it is in a vacuum. Things to be considered are:

Plan versus actual -- if the numbers are what was budgeted and nothing favorable or adverse is occurring, then no time will be wasted on unneeded analysis.

Current year versus last year for the same period report on 13 periods for a monthly metric.

IT Metrics

The metrics for each of the areas are presented in the tables that follow.

Financial

Report	Metrics
Key Measures	**All data is captured for a rolling 13 months** Expenses - Period Actual (Dollars) Expenses - Period Plan (Dollars) Staffing - Period Actual (FTEs[22]) Staffing - Period Plan (FTEs) On-line Availability[23] - Plan (%) On-line Availability - Actual (%) Billing Performance - Plan (Dollars) Billing Performance - Actual (Dollars)
Expense Performance Summary	**All data is captured for a rolling 13 months** Current Period - Actual (Dollars) Current Period - Plan (Dollars) Year to Date - Actual (Dollars) Year to Date - Plan (Dollars) YTD Variance from Plan - Period (Dollars) YTD Variance from Plan - YTD (Dollars)
Expense Variance by Category	**All data is captured for current fiscal year by budget category** Current Period - Plan (Dollars) Current Period - Actual (Dollars) Current Period - Actual (Variance Analysis) Cumulative YTD - Plan (Dollars) Cumulative YTD- Actual (Dollars) Cumulative YTD - Actual (Variance Analysis)
Expense Variance by Cost Center	**All data is captured for current fiscal year by Cost Center** Current Period - Plan (Dollars) Current Period - Actual (Dollars) Current Period - Actual (Variance Analysis) Cumulative YTD - Plan (Dollars) Cumulative YTD- Actual (Dollars) Cumulative YTD - Actual (Variance Analysis)

Figure 19 - Financial Metrics - Part 1 of 2

---

[22]   FTE is Full Time Equivalents

[23]   Some users prefer man hours or revenue lost due to failure of system availability. This is a negative measure and we have opted to show only positive metrics in this set of reports.

Financial (Continued)

Report	Metrics
Capital Plan Performance	**All data is captured for a rolling 13 months** Current Period - Actual (Dollars) Current Period - Plan (Dollars) Year to Date - Actual (Dollars) Year to Date - Plan (Dollars) YTD Variance from Plan - Period (Dollars) YTD Variance from Plan - YTD (Dollars)
Project Capital Expenditures	**All data is captured for project's life** **ITD- Inception to Date** Project Capital - Year to Date (Dollars) Project Capital - Inception to Date (Dollars) Project Capital - Original Plan (Dollars) Project Capital - Current Plan (Dollars) Project Capital - Plan Variance (Dollars)
Billing Allocation	**All data is captured for rolling 13 months** Current Period - Actual (Dollars) Current Period - Plan (Dollars)
System Usage by Customer	**All data is captured for fiscal year** System Usage by Customer - Period (Percent) System Usage by Customer - YTD (Percent)
Resource Usage by Customer	**All data is captured for fiscal year** **(one page per customer)** Usage by Type - Development (Percent) Usage by Type - Support (Percent) Usage by Type - Storage (Percent) Usage by Type - Processing(Percent) Usage by Type - Total (Percent)

Figure 20 - Financial Metrics - Part 2 of 2

Staffing[24]

Report	Metrics

Staff Plan Performance	**All data is captured for a rolling 13 months**
	
	Head Count Actual Vs Plan -
	    Actual Employees (FTE)
	    Actual Contractors (FTE)
	    Employee Plan (FTE)
	Staffing Analysis -
	    Actual Employees (FTE)
	    Actual Contractors (FTE)

Head Count Summary	**All data is captured for current fiscal year** Employees by Cost Center - Plan (FTE) Employees by Cost Center - Actual (FTE) Contractors by Cost Center - Plan (FTE) Contractors by Cost Center - Actual (FTE) Total by Cost Center - Actual (FTE) Total by Cost Center - Plan (FTE) Total Headcount {by Type}- Actual (FTE) Total Headcount {by Type}- Plan (FTE)
Staff Turnover Report	**All data is captured for current fiscal year** YTD Staff Turnover by Department (Percent) YTD Staff Turnover by Department (Count)
Protected Classes Summary	**All data is captured for the current period** Number of Minorities (Single Class) Employees Number of Minorities (Multiple Class) Employees Number of ADA Total Number of Employees

Figure 21 - Staffing Metrics

---

24   All staffing reports are defined in units of Full Time Equivalents (FTEs). A FTE is one employee who works 40 hours per week. An employee who works 50 hours per week is 1.25 FTEs.

Internet[25] - Electronic Infrastructure

Report	Metrics
User Penetration	**All data is captured for a rolling 13 months** Number of Total Users (Plan/Actual) Number of Total User Hours (Plan/Actual) Number Users by Department(Plan/Actual) Number User Hours by Department (Plan/Actual) Cost of External Internet Services (POP Accounts) Cost of External Internet Products (i.e. Databases) FTP Volume (Plan/Actual) Telnet Volume (Plan/Actual) Top Ten Users (Size/Count) Non-Users - Inactive Users
E-mail Traffic	**All data is captured for a rolling 13 months** Internal E-Mail Users (Plan/Actual) Internal E-Mail Messages (Plan/Actual) Inbound External E-Mail Messages/Size Outbound External E-Mail Messages/Size Electronic Post Office Size Top Ten Users (Size/Count/In/Out) Inactive Users Top Ten Oldest Messages Not Opened
USENET Traffic	**All data is captured for a rolling 13 months** USENET User Counts (Plan/Actual) USENET User Hours (Plan/Actual) USENET Transfer Volume (Plan/Actual) USENET Files Size (Plan/Actual) USENET Posting Size (Plan/Actual) USENET Positing Number (Plan/Actual) Largest Thread Size - Enterprise Newsgroups Postings by Number - Enterprise Newsgroups
WEB Site Statistics	**All data is captured for a rolling 13 months** Number of Hits (Plan/Actual) Top Ten WEB Pages Number of Direct Inquiries To Enterprise Number of WEB Page Changes Bottom Ten WEB Pages WEB Page Aging WEB Hits by Hour
Electronic Commerce	**All data is captured for a rolling 13 months** Product Inquiries Via Internet Sales - Number of Orders (Plan/Actual) Sales - Dollar Volume Orders (Plan/Actual) Sales by Product Offering Return Orders - Number (Plan/Actual) Return Orders - Dollars (Plan/Actual) Returns by Product
Volume Users	High Volume Users Low Volume Users

Figure 22 - Internet Metrics

---

25   This same set of metrics should be kept for an enterprise's Internet.

Competitive/Comparative

Report	Metrics
Revenue & Capital	**All data is captured for a rolling 13 months** Expense as Percent of Revenue - Plan (Ratio) Expense as Percent of Revenue - Actual (Ratio) Expense per Customer - Plan (Dollars)[26] Expense per Customer - Actual (Dollars) Capital as Percent of Revenue Plan (Percent) Capital as Percent of Revenue Actual (Percent)

Expenses & Staffing	**All data is captured for a rolling 13 months**
	
	IT vs. Company Expense 3 Month Trend
	    Plan (Percent)
	    Actual (Percent)
	IT vs. Company Staffing 3 Month Trend
	    Plan (Percent)
	    Actual (Percent)
	IT Cost per Company Employee 3 Month Trend
	    Plan (Dollars)
	    Actual (Dollars)

Competitive Application Matrix	**All data is captured for at a point in time**
	
	Key Industry Applications
	    Enterprise Status and Staffing
	    Competitor Status and Staffing
	Technologies Used
	    Enterprise
	    Competitors
	IT Metrics
	    Enterprise Focus
	    Competitors Focus

Technology Penetration Trends	**All data is captured for last 5 quarters** Devices vs. Employees (Number)

Figure 23 - Competitive/Comparative Metrics

---

26   In the case of a company that has 30,000 customers, cost would be Expense per Customer. Some enterprises will use a measure associated with the service provided. In the airline industry a measure used is cost per Revenue Passenger Mile.

Productivity

Report	Metrics

Development Productivity	**All data is captured for a rolling 13 months**
	
	Units of Work[27] - Plan (Count)
	Units of Work - Actual (Count)
	Development Staffing - Headcount (Actual)
	Development Staffing - Headcount (FTE)
	Development Productivity Ratio
	    Units of Work per FTE
	    Units of Work per Actual
	    Units of Work Target

Production Support Productivity	**All data is captured for a rolling 13 months**
	
	Job Processed Plan (Count)
	Jobs Processed Actual (Count)
	Support Staffing - Headcount (Actual)
	Support Staffing - Headcount (FTE)
	Production Productivity Ratio
	    Jobs Processed per FTE
	    Jobs Processed per Actual
	    Jobs Processed Target

Response Time Reports[28]	**All data is captured via monitor or stop watch** Application User Response Time

Figure 24 - Productivity Metrics

---

27   Units of work can be items such as function points. Better measures are a number of events completed by the group such as number of modules moved into production for a development organization or number of phone calls answered by a customer services organization.

28   User Vision of Performance Reports are used as samples -- Note "UVP" is a software product and service of Positive Support Review, Santa Monica, California

System Development

Report	Metrics
Service Request Backlog[29]	**All data is captured for a rolling 13 months** Number of Service Requests - Opened (Count) Number of Service Requests - Closed (Count) Number of Service Requests - Backlog (Count) Backlog - Actual (Number Days) Backlog - Plan (Number Days) Time to Complete Priority 1 (Days) Time to Complete Priority 2 (Days) Time to Complete Priority 3 (Days)

Project Status Report[30]	**All data is captured for life of project**
	
	Detail Budget and Status by Step[31]
	  Man Hours Approved
	  Man Hours Actual
	  Man Hours Estimated to Complete
	  Man Hours Total to Complete
	  Man Hours Variance

Service Request Aging	Age of Service Request Count by Type
Service Request Closure Priority 1	**All data is captured for a rolling 13 months** Priority 1 Service Requests Closed - Actual (Count) Priority 1 Service Requests Closed - Plan (Count)
Service Request Closure Priority 2 and 3	**All data is captured for a rolling 13 months** Priority 2 Service Requests Closed - Actual (Count) Priority 2 Service Requests Closed - Plan (Count) Priority 3 Service Requests Closed - Actual (Count) Priority 3 Service Requests Closed - Plan (Count)
Conversion Status	**All data is captured for a rolling 13 months** Number Records (Value) Number Records Converted (Value) Conversion - Records in Error (Value) Conversion - Projected Error Records (Value)

Figure 25 - System Development Metrics

---

[29] Service requests for purposes of this book are defined as follows:
  Priority 1 -- Must fix now, system will not run
  Priority 2 -- Need to fix soon, user has a work around
  Priority 3 -- Enhancement to the system

[30] We have used man hours as the unit of measure for this to eliminate rate and pricing variances.

[31] Steps for many projects are defined by a company's System Development Methodology (SDM)

Reengineering - Office Automation

Report	Metrics
Reengineered Service Performance	**All data is captured for a rolling 13 months** Number Service Work Orders - Plan (Count) Number Service Work Orders - Actual (Count) Cost of Service - Plan (Dollars) Cost of Service - Actual (Dollars) Cost per Service Order- Plan (Dollars per) Cost per Service Order- Actual (Dollars per)
Home Office Workers	Number of Home Office Worker Hours (Plan/Actual) Number of Home Office E-Mail Messages Number of Home Office Faxes Sent/Received Hours of Paid In Office Parking Miles Home Office Workers Reimbursed

Home Office Productivity	Number of Home Office Work Hours vs.
	    Number of Total Work Hours
	Number of Home Office E-Mail Messages vs.
	    Number of in Office E-Mail Messages
	Number of Home Office Faxes Sent/Received vs.
	    Number of in Offices Faxes Sent/Received

E-Mail Usage	**All data is captured for a rolling 13 months** Number of Inbound Messages Number of Outbound Messages Percentage of Disk Full (Percent)
Voice Mail Usage	**All data is captured for a rolling 13 months** Number of Users Plan Number of Users Actual Percentage of Disk Full (Percent)

Project Status Report	**All data is captured for life of project**
	
	Detail Budget and Status by Step[32]
	    Man Hours Approved
	    Man Hours Actual
	    Man Hours Estimated to Complete
	    Man Hours Total to Complete
	    Man Hours Variance

Figure 26 - Reengineering - Office Automation Metrics

---

[32] Steps for many projects are defined by a company's System Development Methodology (SDM)

Quality Assurance

Report	Metrics

Test Results by Release	<u>All data is captured for a rolling 13 months</u>
	
	Number of Problems Reported
	    Priority 1 (Count)
	    Priority 2 (Count)
	    Priority 3 (Count)
	Number of Problems Resolved
	    Priority 1 (Count)
	    Priority 2 (Count)
	    Priority 3 (Count)
	Number of Problems Outstanding
	    Priority 1 (Count)
	    Priority 2 (Count)
	    Priority 3 (Count)

Release Test Comparison (Special)	<u>Comparison of prior Test Results by Release to see the quality of release versus prior releases</u>
	
	Variance Analysis of Problems Reported Prior Release versus Current Release
	Number of Problems Reported
	    Priority 1 (Variance Count)
	    Priority 2 (Variance Count)
	    Priority 3 (Variance Count)
	Number of Problems Resolved
	    Priority 1 (Variance Count)
	    Priority 2 (Variance Count)
	    Priority 3 (Variance Count)
	Number of Problems Outstanding
	    Priority 1 (Variance Count)
	    Priority 2 (Variance Count)
	    Priority 3 (Variance Count)

Customer Satisfaction Report	<u>All data is captured for a rolling 13 months</u> Number of Customer Complaints Logged Number of Program Discrepancies Logged Number of FTE Hours of System Outage Number of Processing Items Late vs. On-Time
Quality Improvement Program	<u>All data is captured for a rolling 13 months</u> Initial Status of Errors by Type (Count) Current Status of Errors by Type (Count) Problems Outstanding Plan (Count) Problems Outstanding Actual (Count)

Figure 27 - Quality Assurance Metrics

Help Desk

Report	Metrics
Work Load Summary	**All data is captured for a rolling 13 weeks** Call Statistics - Incoming Calls (Count) Call Statistics - Outgoing Calls (Count) Problem Statistics Incidents (Count) Problem Statistics Average/Operator (Count)
Quick Incidents	**All data is captured for a rolling 13 months** Quick Incidents[33] - Incidents (Count) Quick Incidents - Quicks (Count) Quick Incidents - Moving Average (Percent)
Problem Notification Analysis	**All data is captured for current fiscal year** Problem Notification by Source - Period (Count) Problem Notification by Source - YTD (Count) Problem Notification by Customer - Period (Count) Problem Notification by Customer - YTD (Count)

Problem Notification by Priority	**All data is captured for a rolling 13 months**
	
	Number Reported
	    Priority 1 (Count)
	    Priority 2 (Count)
	    Priority 3 (Count)
	Number Closed
	    Priority 1 (Count)
	    Priority 2 (Count)
	    Priority 3 (Count)
	Number Remaining Open
	    Priority 1 (Count)
	    Priority 2 (Count)
	    Priority 3 (Count)

Figure 28 - Help Desk Metrics - Part 1 of 2

---

33   A quick incident is one in which the help desk receives a call and is able to answer the question within 5 minutes with the caller still on the line.

Help Desk (Cont'd)

Report	Metrics

Problem Notification by Category	<u>All data is captured for a rolling 13 months</u>
	
	Number Reported
	    Hardware (Count)
	    Communications / LAN (Count)
	    Office Automation (Count)
	    Software (Count)
	Number Closed
	    Hardware (Count)
	    Communications / LAN (Count)
	    Office Automation (Count)
	    Software (Count)
	Number Remaining Open
	    Hardware (Count)
	    Communications / LAN (Count)
	    Office Automation (Count)
	    Software (Count)

Problem Closure Statistics	<u>All data is captured for a rolling 13 months</u>
	
	Priority 1 - Days to Close 80% (Average)
	Priority 1 - Days to Close All (Average)
	Priority 1 - Days to Close Goal (Average)
	Priority 2 & 3 - Days to Close 80% (Average)
	Priority 2 &3 - Days to Close All (Average)
	Priority 2 & 3 - Days to Close Goal (Average)
	Days to Close Trend
	    Priority 1 (3 Month Moving Average)
	    Priority 2 (3 Month Moving Average)
	    Priority 3 (3 Month Moving Average)

Installation Repair Management	<u>All data is captured for a rolling 13 months</u> Terminal Installations All (Average Days) Terminal Installations 95% (Average Days) Terminal Installations Low (Quickest Days) Terminal Installations High (Longest Days) Terminal Repair All (Average Days) Terminal Repair 95% (Average Days) Terminal Repair Low (Quickest Days) Terminal Repair High (Longest Days) Printer Installations All (Average Days) Printer Installations 95% (Average Days) Printer Installations Low (Quickest Days) Printer Installations High (Longest Days) Printer Repair All (Average Days) Printer Repair 95% (Average Days) Printer Repair Low (Quickest Days) Printer Repair High (Longest Days)

Figure 29 - Help Desk Metrics - Part 2 of 2

Computer Operations

Report	Metrics
Computer Capacity	**All data is captured for a rolling 13 months** CPU[34] Usage - MIPS[35] - Peak (Number) CPU Usage - MIPS - Average (Number) CPU Usage - MIPS - Maximum (Number) CPU Usage - MIPS - Acceptable (Number) DASD[36] Usage - Gigabytes - Maximum (Capacity) DASD Usage - Gigabytes - Actual (Usage)
Combined Computer Work Load	**All data is captured for a rolling 13 months** CPU On-line Transactions - Plan (Count) CPU On-line Transactions - Actual (Count) Batch Production Jobs - Plan (Count) Batch Production Jobs - Actual (Count)
On-Line Performance Summary *See Also Productivity Reports*	**All data is captured for a rolling 13 months** On-Line Availability - Plan (Percent) On-Line Availability - Actual (Percent) On-Line Response Time - Plan (Seconds) On-Line Response Time -Average (Seconds) On-Line Response Time - 90% (Seconds)
E-Mail and EDI Traffic	**All data is captured for a rolling 13 months** Internal E-Mail Messages - Sent/Received External E-Mail Messages - Sent/Received EDI Transactions (Dollars/Count)
Computer Outages	**All data is captured for a rolling 13 months** Number of Outages (Count) Total Outage Time (Minutes) Average Resolution Time - Goal (Minutes) Average Resolution Time - Average (Minutes)
Batch Performance Summary	**All data is captured for a rolling 13 months** Main Batch Processing Performance - Plan (%) Main Batch Processing Performance - Actual (%)
Billing & Report Distribution Performance	**All data is captured for a rolling 13 months** Billing Performance - Days Early/Late Actual Billing Performance - Days Early/Late Plan Reports Delivered on Time Plan (Percent) Reports Delivered on Time Actual (Percent)
Charge Back Details	**All data is captured for current fiscal year** Billings by Department YTD (Percent)

Figure 30 - Computer Operations Metrics

34   CPU -- Central Processing Unit is another term for computer
35   MIPS -- Millions of Instructions Per Second
36   DASD -- Direct Access Storage Device is another term for hard disk storage space and a Gigabyte is 1,000 Megabytes of storage space

Communications

Report	Metrics
Network Outages	**All data is captured for a rolling 13 months** Number of Outages (Count) Total Outage Time (Minutes) Average Resolution Time - Goal (Minutes) Average Resolution Time - Average (Minutes)
Electronic Commerce	**All data is captured for a rolling 13 months** Internal E-Mail Messages - Sent/Received External E-Mail Messages - Sent/Received EDI Transactions (Dollars/Count)
Switch Performance Statistics	**All data is captured for a rolling 13 months** Number of Trunks Busy Plan Number of Trunks Busy Actual Agents on Call Plan Agents on Call Actual
Voice Mail Performance	**All data is captured for a rolling 13 months** Number of Users Plan (Count) Number of Users Actual (Count) Percentage of Disk Full (Percent)

Figure 31 - Communications Metrics

Other - Technology

Report	Metrics
Workstation Analysis	**All data is captured for a rolling 13 months** Number of Workstations - Plan (Count) Number of Workstations - Actual (Count) Workstation Penetration by Department Plan (%) Workstation Penetration by Department Actual (%)
LAN Analysis	**All data is captured for a rolling 13 months** Number of Users - Plan (Count) Number of Users - Actual (Count) Maximum Number of Users- Plan (Count) Maximum Number of Users Actual (Count)
Usage Analysis	**All data is captured for a rolling 13 months** Number - Plan (Count) Number - Actual (Count) Penetration by Department Plan (%) Penetration by Department Actual (%)

Figure 32 - Other - Technology Metrics

Enterprise/Industry Specific

Report	Metrics
Distribution	**All data is captured for a rolling 13 months**
	Quantity Shipped (#Trucks) (Plan/Actual)
	Cost per Unit Shipped (or X000) IT Expense - Plan
	Cost per Unit Shipped (or X000) IT Expense - Actual
	Number Bills of Lading (Plan/Actual)
	Cost Per Bill of Lading (Plan/Actual)
	Service Level Percent (Plan)
	Service Level Actual (Actual)
	Days (or $) Inventory - Received (Plan/Actual)
	Days (or $) Inventory - Shipped (Plan/Actual)
	Days (or $) Inventory - On Hand (Plan/Actual)
	Order/Return Throughput
	Number of Orders Processed
	Number of Returns
	Number of Distribution Orders
	Order/Return Handling
	Orders on Time
	Returns Processed on Time
	Distribution Orders on Time
	Stock/Warehouse/Shipping Performance
	Picking Accuracy
	Bin Level Inventory Accuracy
	Parcel Accuracy
	Percentage Audits Passed
	Timeliness of EDI Transmissions
	On Time EDI Transmissions (TO)
	On Time EDI Transmissions (FROM)
	On Time Reports to Customers
	On Time Scheduled Data Transmission
	Distribution Activity by Production Source (Actual vs. Forecast)
	New Product Orders
	Promotions
	Restocking Orders
	Other Orders
Education	**All data is captured for a rolling 13 months**
	Student Electronic Hours (Plan/Actual)
	Cost per Student (Plan/Actual)
	Number Electronic Transactions (Plan/Actual)
	Number of Electronic Customer Interactions
	Training Quality Goals
	Satisfaction Survey Results
	Average Number of Weeks For Training
	Percentage Completing Training
	Absenteeism Index
	Unused Sick Days
	Unused Vacation Days

Figure 33 - Enterprise/Industry Specific Metrics Part 1 of 4

Enterprise/Industry Specific (cont'd)

Report	Metrics

Entertainment	**All data is captured for a rolling 13 months**
	
	Quantity Shipped (Plan/Actual)
	Cost per Unit Shipped (or X000) IT Expense - Plan
	Cost per Unit Shipped (or X000) IT Expense - Actual
	Number Title (Plan/Actual)
	Cost Per Title (Plan/Actual)
	Service Level Percent (Plan)
	Service Level Actual (Actual)
	Days (or $) Inventory - Received (Plan/Actual)
	Days (or $) Inventory - Shipped (Plan/Actual)
	Days (or $) Inventory - On Hand (Plan/Actual)
	Title Performance
	    Year to Date Unit Shipments
	    Inception to Date Unit Shipments
	    Net Unit Sales – Titles (Inventory) Assets (Net of Returns)

Financial Service	**All data is captured for a rolling 13 months**
	
	Number Transactions (Plan/Actual)
	Cost per Transaction(or X000) IT Expense - Plan
	Cost per Transaction (or X000) IT Expense - Actual
	Dollar Volume Electronic Transactions (Plan/Actual)
	Average Size of Electronic Transaction (Plan/Actual)
	Service Level Percent (Plan)
	Service Level Actual (Actual)
	Number E-Mail Messages Inbound
	Number E-Mail Messages Outbound
	Customer Satisfaction
	    Satisfaction Index
	    Percentage of Repeat Customers This Period
	    Percentage of Customer With No Activity
	      in the Last Two Periods
	    Repeat Customer - Order Size Larger
	      Current Period Versus Prior Period

Government	**All data is captured for a rolling 13 months** Customer Count (Plan/Actual) Cost per Customer (Plan/Actual) Dollar Volume (Plan/Actual) Number Electronic Transactions (Plan/Actual) Dollar Volume Electronic Transactions (Plan/Actual Number of Electronic Customer Interactions WEB Page Inquires E-Mail Volume

Figure 34 - Enterprise/Industry Specific Metrics Part 2 of 4

Enterprise/Industry Specific   (cont'd)

Report	Metrics

Hospitality	**All data is captured for a rolling 13 months**
	
	Customer Count (Plan/Actual)
	Dollar Volume (Plan/Actual)
	Cost per Customer (Plan/Actual)
	Number Electronic Transactions (Plan/Actual)
	Dollar Volume Electronic Transactions (Plan/Actual
	Number of Electronic Customer Interactions
	Customer Satisfaction Index
	    Customer Counts
	    Repeat Customers
	    Customer Credits
	    Sales
	    Customer Service Complaints

Insurance	**All data is captured for a rolling 13 months**
	
	Number Transactions (Plan/Actual)
	Cost per Transaction(or X000) IT Expense - Plan
	Cost per Transaction (or X000) IT Expense - Actual
	Dollar Volume Electronic Transactions (Plan/Actual)
	Average Size of Electronic Transaction (Plan/Actual)
	Service Level Percent (Plan)
	Service Level Actual (Actual)
	Number E-Mail Messages Inbound
	Number E-Mail Messages Outbound
	Business Supported
	    Number of Lines of Insurance Supported
	    Cost per Policy per Line of Business
	    Number of Days Required to Process Various
	        Claims (Simple, Average, Complex)
	    Number of Employees per Policy per
	        Line of Business

Manufacturing	**All data is captured for a rolling 13 months**
	
	Quantity Manufactured (Plan/Actual)
	Number Production Orders (Plan/Actual)
	Number Orders Late/Under (Plan/Actual)
	Cost per Unit (Or X000) IT Expense - Plan
	Cost per Unit (Or X000) IT Expense - Actual
	Service Level Percent (Plan)
	Service Level Actual (Actual)
	Days (or $) Inventory - Raw Material (Plan/Actual)
	Days (or $) Inventory - In Process (Plan/Actual)
	Days (or $) Inventory - Finished Goods (Plan/Actual)
	Manufacturing Goals
	    Manufacturing Defect Returns
	    Scrap
	    Machine Down Time
	    Set-Up Variances
	    Production Quality - % Products Returned
	        For Rework
	    Production Quality - % Products Rejected by
	        Customers

Figure 35 - Enterprise/Industry Specific Metrics Part 3 of 4

Enterprise/Industry Specific (cont'd)

Report	Metrics

Medical	**All data is captured for a rolling 13 months**
	
	Patient Days Count (Plan/Actual)
	Dollar Volume by Department (Plan/Actual)
	Cost per Patient (Plan/Actual)
	Number Electronic Transactions (Plan/Actual)
	Dollar Volume Electronic Transactions (Plan/Actual
	Number of Electronic Customer Interactions
	Quantity of Service Provided
	    Number of Patient Days
	    Number of Lab Tests by Department
	    Number of Complaints
	    Number of Encounters

Real Estate	**All data is captured for a rolling 13 months**
	
	Number Leases/Sales (Plan/Actual)
	Cost per Lease/Sale (or X000) IT Expense - Plan
	Cost per Lease/Sale (or X000) IT Expense - Actual
	Dollar Volume Electronic Transactions (Plan/Actual)
	Average Size of Electronic Transaction (Plan/Actual)
	Service Level Percent (Plan)
	Service Level Actual (Actual)
	Number E-Mail Messages Inbound
	Number E-Mail Messages Outbound
	Volume of Business
	    Number of New Agreements Signed
	    Number and Dollar Value of Sales
	    Square Footage Available to Lease

Retail	**All data is captured for a rolling 13 months**
	
	Customer Count (Plan/Actual)
	Dollar Volume by Product Line (Plan/Actual)
	Cost Per Customer (Plan/Actual)
	Number Electronic Transactions (Plan/Actual)
	Dollar Volume Electronic Transactions (Plan/Actual)
	Number of Electronic Customer Interactions
	Customer Satisfaction
	    Combined Customer Satisfaction Index
	    Missed Due Dates for Order Processing
	    Returns Disposition (Turn-Around Time)
	    Credit Disposition (Turn-Around Time)
	Warehouse Goals
	    Inventory Accuracy - % Locations At 99.5%
	    Average Cycle Time - Time to Re-Stock
	    On Time Shipped Orders
	    Number of Returns Authorized Above Targets

Figure 36 - Enterprise/Industry Specific Metrics Part 4 of 4

Metric Implementation

The implementation process for this type of reporting system needs the support of all levels of management within both IT and the user community. Once the first step of implementing metrics is taken then the second and most important step, the implementation of Service Level Agreements (SLAs), can be taken.

To help you implement SLAs we have defined a process you can follow to implement both a good metric reporting system and SLAs. The implementation process is continual.

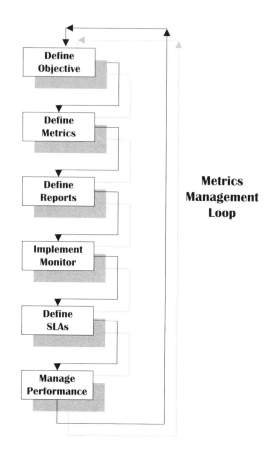

Figure 37 - Implementation Process

Metrics Management Loop

The metrics management loop is a continual management process. Once you have some information you know more. You will need different data. When you start you do not know what you do not know.

A good metrics system will lead you from one metric to another. It will lead insightful individuals to ask many "what if" questions.

| Rule 1 | Once a metric provides less value than the cost of capture, eliminate it |

As you start this process, do not over commit. At the same time, provide your audience with information that can show value or lack thereof. It is to easy to say that metrics will answer all the service level problems of IT. That is not the case.

| Rule 2 | Implement metrics and reporting to set a base line of service |

It is easy for an IT professional to make mistakes in responding to an upset customer or agitated management that wants the "head of someone" who is not performing.

> *A senior executive of an insurance company said that his customer had mandated improved service levels. In response to this the executive and his customer were about to sign a new SLA. This executive was in a quandary as to what to do. He did not know what his customer meant by improved service level. What he did know was that he had a system that was designed for 5 users and now it had 50; response time for an enrollment process was over 14 seconds (the worst that we had ever seen); the revenue generated by the 50 users was providing the company $180,000 of new incremental revenue each month; and the IT professional had no idea whether the changes that were being developed would improve customer service and by how much.*

| Rule 3 | Do not agree to a SLA until you have a good metric, measurement technique and reporting mechanism |

To meet the requirement of the three rules depicted above we have found the multiple step process that is briefly discussed below works well.

Step 1   *Review and evaluate any and all existing metrics, performance and service level reporting that is in place within the enterprise.*

Conduct in depth interviews and have IT's customers and staff identify the critical measures to be reported. Through these interviews, obtain an understanding of the information needs for both internal and external audiences. Evaluate the content and purpose of existing reports. Identify the likely sources of data, and determine how the data is presently collected and maintained.

Step 2. *Identify strengths and weaknesses of the existing reporting and metrics systems.*

Assess how the existing reporting impacts the organization. This includes understanding the adequacy and usefulness of the existing information and report formats. Review observations, findings and recommendations with all levels of the internal and external audiences frequently.

Step 3. *Prepare recommended improvements to the existing reporting program including new service measures.*

Draft new or revised report layouts incorporating appropriate measures for resource utilization, operational performance, and service level reporting to clients. For each report, document the sources of information and suggested report formats. Prepare recommendations on the necessary steps to expand/modify the management reporting program.

Step 4. *Define new and revised reporting programs and prototype selected measures.*

Prepare prototype reports (see Sample Reports) using representative data, or where available, real data. Each prototype report should be designed to facilitate the reader's understanding of its purpose, content, and use. Example reports should be used where prototype reports were not prepared. All reports should be reviewed with personnel who prepare or receive the reports.

Step 5 *Implement and monitor graphic based metrics and use them as a basis for SLAs.*

Implement new and revised metrics and reporting formats with a more graphical approach to displaying information. It is suggested that this be done in the following sequence:

- ❐ Executive reporting
- ❐ SLA reporting - accomplish this after executive reporting package is completed.
- ❐ Other IT reporting for the top IT management and their direct reports. This includes special trend

analysis reporting for senior IT management and standard reports for the larger IT functional units.

❑ Assign a person to be responsible for assembling and producing service level and performance reports. Formalize the data collection responsibilities within each IT functional unit. Eventually data collection should be automated where feasible, such as in the help desk function.

As a result of conducting this process for a number of various clients we have identified several typical deficiencies. The rankings depict the percentage of time we have found them when we conducted such reviews.

Typical Reporting Deficiencies	Rank
Historical reporting further back than six months is not possible due to inconsistent or unavailable data: 1. Equipment / software inventory, 2. Capital budgeting, and 3. Project status reporting.	1
Reasonable data collection and reporting but much of the present reporting is very detailed on the wrong metrics.	2
Service level agreement (SLA) reporting appears to be more important in the near term than it was when the reporting project began. Little value added due to poor design.	3
Internal reporting is formalized, but inconsistent.	4
Reporting activities are mis-aligned	5
Little or no project planning systems to support project management and reporting.	6
While many functions have a responsibility for meeting SLA performance goals, a central focal point was not clearly established for reporting performance and interfacing with the market executive.	7
Little or no traditional project status reporting.	8
Little or no formal time keeping system to support project status reporting.	9

Figure 38 - Reporting Deficiencies

Rule 4	**Begin reporting in areas where reasonable and consistent data is available. Do not produce reports containing questionable historical data or prepare reports without history. Build historical data up over a period of time.**

Once a SLA is agreed to, provide the agreed upon level of service. If a user is not happy with a service level make sure to explain the cost associated with achieving that level. If you provide more service than that agreed to and IT costs are higher than agreed to the user may balk at paying.

Rule 5	**If you provide better service than agreed to, continually inform your user that costs may go up (to maintain that service level in the future) or service may go down (to keep costs flat).**

IT Report Package

The IT report package presented here consists of approximately 50 reports and over 150 metrics. These reports cover IT's financial, staffing, and operational performance. It covers reporting required under the SLAs. It also includes information on project backlogs and status of the major active projects.

The individual reports in the IT reporting package were designed for multiple audiences. The four primary audiences are:

❒ **IT Senior Management** --
Chief Information Officer and his/her staff.

❒ **IT Operating Group Management** -- IT Management for overall performance and service level for major IT functions and, to report the significant details supporting the total, highlighting trends in critical measures.

❒ **Enterprise Senior Management** -- To report overall performance and service level for IT's total operation.

❒ **Customer Operating Group Management** --
Market Management to report IT's performance and

service level for each market or business unit in accordance with the SLA contracts.

The reports can be assembled into other reporting packages depending on the purpose of the presentation and the audience. In general, there is no need to redevelop reports for different presentations.

The various reporting packages can be electronically assembled. Using this approach, all reports for a given presentation could be printed at one time including a package cover and table of contents. As needed, other information such as supporting schedules can be electronically collated into the reporting package. Alternatively, supporting materials can be manually collated in or manually appended to the back of a report package.

A summary level work plan to implement metrics to support SLAs would include at least the following major tasks.

❏ Initialize the metrics database files for production operations.

❏ Prepare a comprehensive data dictionary for prototype reports and prepare a draft of management procedures.

❏ Formalize data collection procedures and notify persons responsible for supplying the data.

❏ Initialize data collection for production processing.

❏ Design and develop automated interfaces between the metrics databases and existing IT databases.

❏ Begin initial production processing.

❏ Implement consistent performance and service level reporting at all organizational levels within IT; develop additional reports as needed.

❏ Refine performance and service level measures changing service level targets to stimulate continued improvement in IT operations.

SLA Report Package

In the course of developing SLAs for the enterprise it is important to communicate the service level that the user is receiving. Using the IT Report package as a basis let us suggest the sets of reports that should be included with the SLAs.

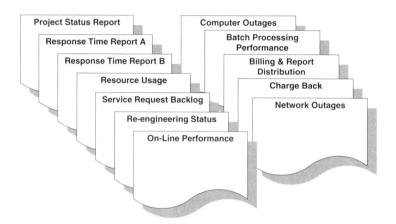

Figure 39 - Reporting Package

With this subset of reports the SLAs can be defined, standards agreed to, implemented and monitored. Other reports could be included, but this is probably more than most organizations have in place today.

The formal SLA should be signed by both the user and IT management. The agreement should contain at least the following components:

- ❐ Processing volume statistics in user terms.
- ❐ Cost for a period of time based on whatever pricing method is agreed to by all parties.
- ❐ Forecast of each of the metrics in the SLA reporting package.
- ❐ Performance standards.
- ❐ Terms and conditions for performance and non-performance by both parties.

This is not an all inclusive list but it is one that covers most of the components that we have seen in organizations that have implemented a successful SLA process.

Data Capture

In order to understand the issues associated with service level or the User's Vision of Performance (UVP) the reader needs to grasp the magnitude of processing a transaction. Let us assume that a user wants to inquire into a database. From the graphic that follows you can see the levels of interaction that must take place.

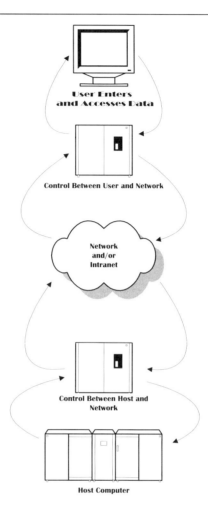

Figure 40 - Control Points

The processing goes all the way from the user to host and back to user at completion. Between each point there is a handshake and some processing that takes place.

With this level of complexity there is a normal target of "sub-second" response time for users. If the IT organization delivers this the discussion that follows is moot.

What is User Vision of Performance

The user's perception of performance (UVP) is how IT is perceived, not how IT professionals measure their performance. UVP is from the moment that the user of the system hits the enter key until the moment in time that the user can execute some other function.

IT professionals often times will say the performance (or response time) is from when the data arrives into the network cloud until it is ready to leave the cloud and go to the user. Most IT functions have tools that measure that response time. What they fail to measure is the interaction of the application, data, network and the user.

Often times the service level that is reported to the user by IT professionals is of internal transaction times (multiple transactions make up a single user interaction with the system); database input output counts (multiple input output accesses to the database are common for a single user transaction -- we have found instances where there are over 100 accesses to a database for a single user transaction); and events not comprehended by the user (EXCPs or other such data).

Monitors

One simple answer that you may try is to install either a hardware or software monitor. These are devices that capture the number of events that have occurred and/or the time associated with a particular event. If, for example, you put a monitor on the CPU you can capture data on all events that start or pass through it. If you put a monitor on the database controller you can measure counts on database access as well as the time to complete the event.

That sounds wonderful, but there are limitations. If a monitor is a passive one (typically an external hardware monitor) you normally will not be able to tie the counts and timings to other than hardware events. That means if there are multiple applications running in the CPU you will be unable to tell how well the CPU is optimized.

Put another way, it would be like saying the internal combustion engine is running at a rate where it is consuming 22 gallons of gasoline per mile. You would not be able to know that you are traveling at 55 miles per hour going east on highway I-10 to your mother's house on Christmas Eve. If what you wanted to know was how much gasoline you were consuming, that would be okay.

Hardware Monitors

There are reasons to use these but there are limitations the user must understand. Below is a table listing the advantages and disadvantages of Hardware Monitors.

Hardware Monitors	
Advantages	**Disadvantages**
1. Typically does not take any resources away from the device being monitored	1. Difficult to correlate events measured with application activities
2. Devices are single purpose and can give much data on the item being measured	2. Measurement cost very high if used on devices that are dispersed such as workstations
3. Reporting is very concise	3. Reporting does not correlate to easily defined non technical terms
	4. Requires significant expertise to analyze data and understand what it all means

Figure 41 - Hardware Monitors

Given this, care should be used in trying to apply the information that is being captured. For example, if a hardware monitor is put on the control unit (B) between the user (A) and the Network (C) you will still have a number of blind spots.

❑ The overhead associated with the "handshake" between the user device and the control unit.

❑ The overhead associated with the network (C); the network controller (D); the CPU (E); the database controller (F); and the database (Groups).

You will know how many events passed by the controller. But how many of those events were a person just hitting the enter key versus some unit of work?

Software Monitors

The software monitors normally reside on the CPU and capture data at that level. They do offer a number of primary advantages but at a significant cost. Software monitors normally can take up to 25% to 30% of the total system resources to run.

Software Monitors			
Advantages		**Disadvantages**	
1.	Easier to correlate events measured with application activities	1.	Typically takes significant resources away from the device being monitored
2.	Reporting can correlate to easily defined non technical terms	2.	Measurement cost very high if used on devices that are dispersed such as workstations
3.	Reporting can be very concise if defined well	3.	Measurement does not typically provide a total view -- see discussion earlier
4.	Devices are multiple purpose and can give much data on the item being measured	4.	Requires significant expertise to analyze data and understand what it all means
		5.	Costly to purchase or lease

Figure 42 - Software Monitors

If response time is poor, once you add the software monitor response time becomes unbearable. The process you would go through to understand where you were would make your user even more unhappy. Are you sure you want to do that?

Emulation Monitors

These are typically software monitors that emulate system performance. One such product is UVP that is sold by Positive Support Review. The program runs on a device (a PC) that looks like a user terminal. It sends transactions every x seconds to the CPU and exercises the database. There are a number of advantages as well as disadvantages to this approach.

Emulation Monitors	
Advantages	**Disadvantages**
1. Easier to correlate events measured with application activities	1. Requires significant expertise to write scripts that work
2. Reporting can correlate to easily defined non technical terms	2. Measurement does not typically provide a total view -- see discussion above
3. Reporting is very concise if defined well	3. Design is limited to features and functions implemented in the software
4. Multiple purpose and can give much data on the item being measured	4. Changes in operating systems such as version upgrades often need changes to be implemented in the emulation software
5. Takes minimal resources away from the system	
6. Requires limited expertise to analyze data and understand	
7. Inexpensive to purchase	

Figure 43 - Emulation Monitors

Classes of transactions can be monitored and typical response times can be calculated and displayed in real time. This allows for immediate feedback to the user. Some additional points to note on UVP are:

❐ As new features are implemented objective performance improvement results (if any) can be quickly tabulated.

❐ Volume testing can be generated for new applications to show what the expected response time is given a certain number of users.

❐ Network overhead can be calculated easily.

❐ Monitoring can be done remotely and analysis of results done centrally.

❐ Captured data can be reprocessed in a time lapsed mode.

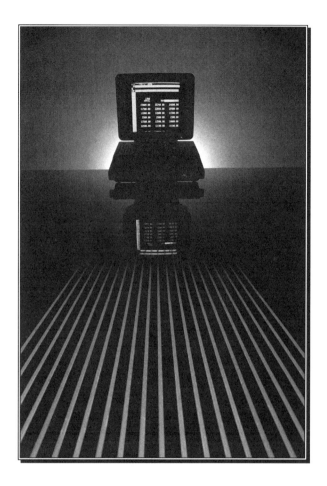

Metrics System

To assist enterprises in developing a quality metrics reporting package, Positive Support Review has developed a software package specifically for this purpose. This system was used to produce most of the reports that are shown in this book. PSR's Metrics HandiGuide® software, when used in conjunction with Excel and Word for Windows, will produce all the metrics reports shown in the sample report section of this book *(see Sample Reports)*. What follows is a brief description of how the system works. If the reader has not purchased this system you can skip this chapter. There are instructions in the back of the book on how to acquire this system.

Overview

Assuming that the reader has reviewed all of the metrics and reports that are discussed in this book, the reader should be able to follow a very simple process to create a management reporting system for their organization.

Producing these metrics with this reporting package is an easy five step process:

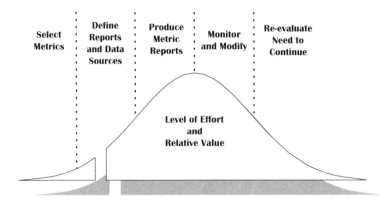

Figure 44 - Metric Life Cycle

Metrics will cause behavior to be modified. Once it is modified one of the things that you should do is eliminate the metric after the value to capture and report the data exceeds the value in business terms.

One word of caution, if the reader just implements all of the reports and metrics as depicted in this book -- **the reader will fail in meeting the enterprises reporting requirements**. Care should be taken to identify those metrics and reports that will best meet the organization's business need.

Select Metrics

As you start the process the reader needs to select the reports that they will want to produce. Each of the ones that we have defined has some prototype data element defined. Each of these will need to be evaluated and then processed to capture the initial data. Once this is done a preliminary estimate of the time and effort necessary to capture the data can be defined. Do not be surprised to find that some of the data will be too costly or cumbersome to capture and report while other data will already be available.[37]

The first step toward producing your comprehensive metrics reporting package is selecting the individual reports to be included. Not all enterprises need every report included with the system. The Metrics HandiGuide® Software has a report selection screen that allows the user to customize the reporting package by selecting only those reports which are relevant to their organization.

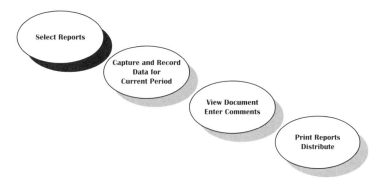

Figure 45 - Select Reports

With this system the way you select a report is to place an "X" in the box next to the report name. Once this page is completed, click on "more" and you will proceed through all of the options. When finished, the system will generate the shell for the reports and metrics discussed in this book.

Full documentation on the use of the system is provided when it is purchased. This discussion is only intended as a brief overview.

Capture and Record Data for Current Period

Once the appropriate reports have been selected, the system will provide a series of prompts for the data to be included. Once data is entered, it is stored in the system's database for future use. In this way, reports that contain trend charts do not require data to be re-entered from previous periods. Only the current period's data is required for

---

37   If the data already exists in various computer systems, have your IT group export the data from your existing systems and import it into the Metrics Access Data Bases.

trend charts. The system has been programmed to chart the proper data.

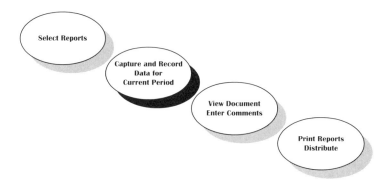

Figure 46 - Capture and Record Data

The system will go from report to report asking for data. In the normal monthly process the user will just have to add the current period result.

The user will be prompted for input through a series of forms. After the data is entered, the system updates all graphs and documents. Each data element can be used on multiple reports. Please refer to the naming conventions. If necessary, these files can be customized by the user with the aid of PSR's programming documentation.

At the completion of the process the system will save the entire report with a name that follows this naming convention.

YYYYMMDD.DOC

Where YYYY is year, MM is month, and DD is date. In this way, multiple versions of the report can be generated without destroying the old history.

View Documents

Once all data has been entered, the system will automatically create a master document incorporating all the reports selected. You may view the document on the screen or print a hard copy to review before finalizing. In order to view the document open it in Word for Windows.

After evaluation, commentary may be necessary to explain various trends and comparisons. You may then use the word processor to enter text in the "discussion boxes" provided on each report page.

Please note that if you generate a new report with updated data, the commentary will have to be copied from one document to another. The system has a series of macros to help do this.

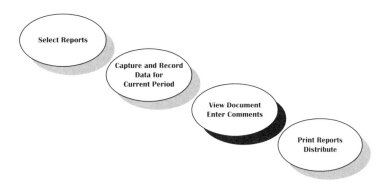

Figure 47 - View Documents and Comment

Print Reports

After adding the necessary commentary, your reporting package is complete. Merely print the final report and distribute to the appropriate parties!

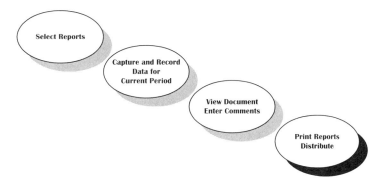

Figure 48 - Print Reports and Distribute

System Modifications

Once metrics are defined for an enterprise, specific changes will need to be made to the metrics and reports. At that time you will need someone who knows Word for Windows and Access.

Technical Naming Conventions

In the Metrics System and this book, we have followed naming conventions for the reports and documents that are produced. Below you will find the naming as it is defined in this book and that system. You will notice the technical name is the upper right hand corner of each discussion box. We suggest you leave that description there if you use the Metrics system to produce the reports.

The **Description** is the description of the report in the Metrics system. On some report name descriptions the word "IT" has been excluded as a prefix for ease of using the list that follows. The column titled **Documents** lists the name of the *.Doc files as used by Word for Windows.

Description	Documents
Text	
Table of Contents	toc.doc
Master Document	master.doc
Summary Information	summary.doc
Financial	
Key Measures Report	1-1.doc
Expense Performance Summary	1-2.doc
Expense Variance by Category	1-3.doc
Expense Variance by Cost Center	1-4.doc
Capital Plan Performance	1-5.doc
Project Capital Expenditures	1-6.doc
Billing Allocation	1-7.doc
System Usage by Customer	1-8.doc
Resource Usage by Customer	1-9.doc
Staffing	
Staff Plan Performance	2-1.doc
Head Count Summary	2-2.doc
Staff Turnover Report	2-3.doc
Protected Classes Summary	2-4.doc

Internet - Electronic Infrastructure

User Penetration Count	3-1.doc
User Penetration Volume	3-2.doc
E-mail Traffic	3-3.doc
USENET Traffic	3-4.doc
WEB Statistics	3-5.doc
Electronic Commerce Sales	3-6.doc
Electronic Commerce Returns	3-7.doc
High Volume Users	3-8.doc
Low Volume Users	3-9.doc

Competitive/Comparative

Revenue & Capital	4-1.doc
Expenses & Staffing	4-2.doc
Competitive Application Matrix	4.3.doc
Technology Penetration Trends	4-4.doc

Productivity

Development Productivity	5-1.doc
Production Support Productivity	5-2.doc
Response Time Reports - A	5-3.doc
Response Time Reports - B	5-4.doc

System Development

Service Request Backlog	6-1.doc
Project Status Report	6-2.doc
Service Request Aging	6-3.doc
Service Request Closure - 1	6-4.doc
Service Request Closure - 2&3	6-5.doc
Conversion Status	6-6.doc

Reengineering - Office Automation

Reengineering Service Performance	7-1doc
Home Office Workers	7-2.doc
Home Office Productivity	7-3.doc
E-Mail Usage	7-4.doc
Voice Mail Usage	7-5.doc
Project Status Report	7-6.doc

Quality Assurance

Test Results by Release	8-1.doc
Release Test Comparison (Special)	8-2.doc
Customer Satisfaction	8-3.doc
Quality Improvement Program	8-4.doc

Help Desk

Work Load Summary	9-1.doc
Quick Incidents	9-2.doc
Problem Notification Analysis	9-3.doc
Problem Notification by Priority	9-4.doc
Problem Notification by Category	9-5.doc
Problem Closure Statistics	9-6.doc
Installation Repair Management	9-7.doc

Computer Operations

Computer Capacity	10-1.doc
Combined Computer Work Load	10-2.doc
On-Line Performance Summary	10-3.doc
E-Mail and EDI Traffic	10-4.doc
Computer Outages	10-5.doc
Batch Processing Performance	10-6.doc
Billing & Report Distribution Perform.	10-7.doc
Charge Back Details	10-8.doc

Communications

Network Outages	11-1.doc
Electronic Commerce	11-2.doc
Switch Performance Report	11-3.doc
Voice Mail Performance	11-4.doc

Other - Technology

Workstation Analysis	12-1.doc
LAN Analysis	12-2.doc
Usage analysis	12-3.doc

Industry Specific[38]

Distribution	13-1.doc
Education	13-2.doc
Entertainment	13-3.doc
Financial Service	13-4.doc
Government	13-5.doc
Hospitality	13-6.doc
Insurance	13-7.doc
Manufacturing	13-8.doc
Medical	13-9.doc
Real Estate	13-10.doc
Retail	13-11.doc

System Requirements

In order to produce the reports and metrics that are presented in this book you will require a reasonably powerful PC. Below are listed the requirements for a PC to run Positive Support Review's IT Metric system.

- ❏ Pentium or greater micro processor
- ❏ 75 MHz or greater preferred
- ❏ 16 MB of RAM
- ❏ Microsoft Windows 95, NT 3.51 or NT 4.0
- ❏ Microsoft Word 7.0 or higher
- ❏ Laser Printer (600 dpi preferred)

---

38   This set of reports have been numbered in a way to provide cross industry uniqueness and is not mandatory.

Sample Reports

Sample Reports

In this section of the book, sample PSR Metrics HandiGuide Reports are presented. Each report has a brief description followed by the report. In the discussion that follows the reader is reminded that individual reports in the IT reporting package were designed for multiple audiences. The four primary audiences are:

- ❐ **IT Senior Management** -- Chief Information Officer (CIO) and his/her staff.

- ❐ **IT Operating Group Management** -- IT Management for overall performance and service level for major IT functions and, to report the significant details supporting the total, highlighting trends in critical measures.

- ❐ **Enterprise Senior Management** (Executive Management and Corporate Executive Committee) -- To report overall performance and service levels for IT's total operation

- ❐ **Customer Operating Group Management** -- Market Management to report IT's performance and service level for each market or business unit in accordance with the SLA contracts.

On the following pages you will find a Table of Contents for all of the report samples that are contained in this chapter of the book.

Report Table of Contents

Financial

Staffing

Internet - Electronic Infrastructure

Competitive/Comparative

Productivity

System Development

Reengineering - Office Automation

Quality Assurance

Help Desk

Computer Operations

Communications

Other

Industry Specific

Key Measures Report

This overview report shows IT Expenses, IT Staffing, On-Line Availability and Billing Performance. As this is a summary report, all information reflected in the four graphs is contained elsewhere in the reporting package. This report is intended initially for the CIO only; however, it may be used in presentations to executive management.

The data for this report is copied from other reports. There is no need for additional data entries. Refer to the other reports which contain the details of the summary data. The comments therein apply to this report as well.

Many organizations place some industry specific measures on this report. For example, one entertainment client includes the number of CD's shipped as a key metric of volume. In another case, a manufacturing company list the cost of IT per finished good item. In this way this report becomes the overall report card for the cost and value of IT to the enterprise.

Metrics
◆ Expenses - Period Actual (Dollars)
◆ Expenses - Period Plan (Dollars)
◆ Staffing - Period Actual (FTEs[39])
◆ Staffing - Period Plan (FTEs)
◆ On-line Availability[40] - Plan (%)
◆ On-line Availability - Actual (%)
◆ Billing Performance - Plan (Dollars)
◆ Billing Performance - Actual (Dollars)

---

[39] FTE is Full Time Equivalents

[40] Some users prefer man hours or revenue lost due to failure of system availability. This is a negative measure and we have opted to show only positive metrics in this set of reports.

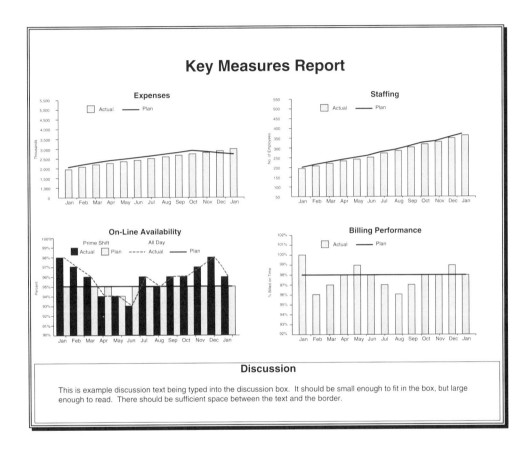

Expense Performance Summary

This report shows the IT performance against the original expense plan. Both current period and year-to-date performances are shown. The variances for current period and year-to-date are reflected in the bottom graph. This report is intended for the CIO to present to the Executive Committee. A similar report will be produced for each of the large cost centers within the IT department.

This report reflects actual IT expenses and the expense budgets. The numbers do not reflect allocations.

Metrics
♦ Current Period - Actual (Dollars)
♦ Current Period - Plan (Dollars)
♦ Year to Date - Actual (Dollars)
♦ Year to Date - Plan (Dollars)
♦ YTD Variance from Plan - Period (Dollars)
♦ YTD Variance from Plan - YTD (Dollars)

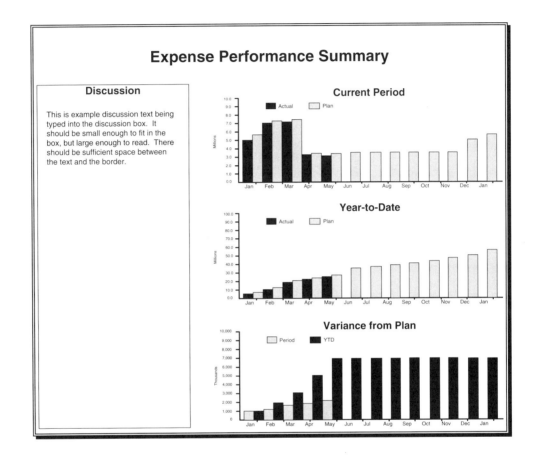

Expense Performance Summary

Discussion

This is example discussion text being typed into the discussion box. It should be small enough to fit in the box, but large enough to read. There should be sufficient space between the text and the border.

Current Period

Year-to-Date

Variance from Plan

Expense Variance by Category

This report shows expense variances by major budget categories for IT in total. This monthly report provides a chart of the plan and actual for each category. Both current period and year-to-date information are provided. For each account the significant variances will be explained in the text frame on the right side of the report. Minor variances below a certain dollar or percentage amount will be summarized in a category called miscellaneous. For the miscellaneous line item no explanation is required on this report.

Because the client performs an in-depth variance analysis each month, it may be necessary to split this report into two pages. One page would show current period data and the second page would show year-to-date data. Alternatively, the high level summary can be produced on a single page showing both current period and year-to-date and attached to this one page report would be a detailed listing of the variances in the format that is used currently within the IT department.

Metrics
♦ Current Period - Plan (Dollars)
♦ Current Period - Actual (Dollars)
♦ Current Period - Actual (Variance Analysis)
♦ Cumulative YTD - Plan (Dollars)
♦ Cumulative YTD- Actual (Dollars)
♦ Cumulative YTD - Actual (Variance Analysis)

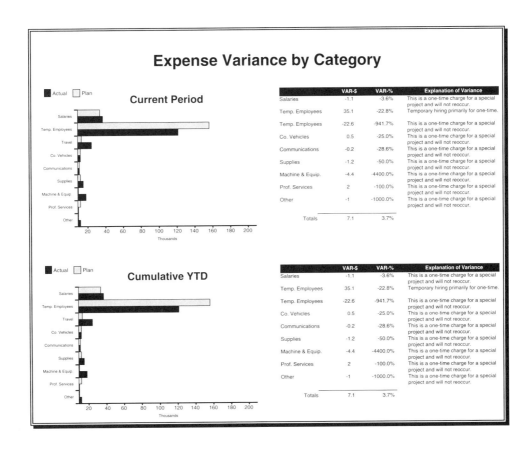

Expense Variance by Category

Current Period

	VAR-$	VAR-%	Explanation of Variance
Salaries	-1.1	-3.6%	This is a one-time charge for a special project and will not reoccur.
Temp. Employees	35.1	-22.8%	Temporary hiring primarily for one-time.
Temp. Employees	-22.6	-941.7%	This is a one-time charge for a special project and will not reoccur.
Co. Vehicles	0.5	-25.0%	This is a one-time charge for a special project and will not reoccur.
Communications	-0.2	-28.6%	This is a one-time charge for a special project and will not reoccur.
Supplies	-1.2	-50.0%	This is a one-time charge for a special project and will not reoccur.
Machine & Equip.	-4.4	-4400.0%	This is a one-time charge for a special project and will not reoccur.
Prof. Services	2	-100.0%	This is a one-time charge for a special project and will not reoccur.
Other	-1	-1000.0%	This is a one-time charge for a special project and will not reoccur.
Totals	7.1	3.7%	

Cumulative YTD

	VAR-$	VAR-%	Explanation of Variance
Salaries	-1.1	-3.6%	This is a one-time charge for a special project and will not reoccur.
Temp. Employees	35.1	-22.8%	Temporary hiring primarily for one-time.
Temp. Employees	-22.6	-941.7%	This is a one-time charge for a special project and will not reoccur.
Co. Vehicles	0.5	-25.0%	This is a one-time charge for a special project and will not reoccur.
Communications	-0.2	-28.6%	This is a one-time charge for a special project and will not reoccur.
Supplies	-1.2	-50.0%	This is a one-time charge for a special project and will not reoccur.
Machine & Equip.	-4.4	-4400.0%	This is a one-time charge for a special project and will not reoccur.
Prof. Services	2	-100.0%	This is a one-time charge for a special project and will not reoccur.
Other	-1	-1000.0%	This is a one-time charge for a special project and will not reoccur.
Totals	7.1	3.7%	

Expense Variance by Cost Center

This monthly report is similar to the IT Variances by Category report except it breaks down the plan and actual by IT Cost Center. For each account the significant variances will be explained in the text frame on the right side of the report. Minor variances below a certain dollar or percentage amount will be summarized in a category called miscellaneous. For the miscellaneous line item no explanation is required on this report.

Because the client performs an in-depth variance analysis each month, it may be necessary to split this report into two pages. One page would show current period data and the second page would show year-to-date data. Alternatively, the high level summary can be produced on a single page showing both current period and year-to-date and attached to this one page report would be a detailed listing of the variances in the format that is used currently within the IT department.

Metrics
◆ Current Period - Plan (Dollars)
◆ Current Period - Actual (Dollars)
◆ Current Period - Actual (Variance Analysis)
◆ Cumulative YTD - Plan (Dollars)
◆ Cumulative YTD- Actual (Dollars)
◆ Cumulative YTD - Actual (Variance Analysis)

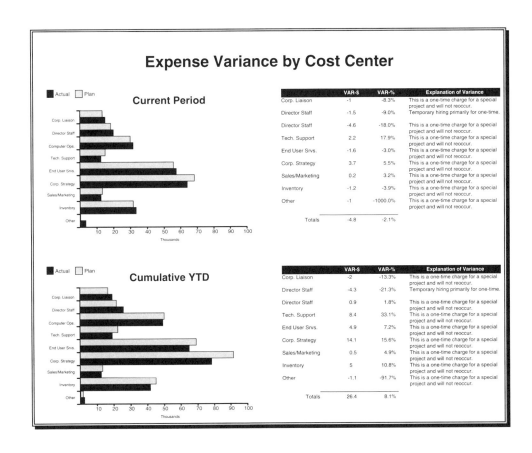

Expense Variance by Cost Center

Current Period

Actual ☐ Plan

	VAR-$	VAR-%	Explanation of Variance
Corp. Liaison	-1	-8.3%	This is a one-time charge for a special project and will not reoccur.
Director Staff	-1.5	-9.0%	Temporary hiring primarily for one-time.
Director Staff	-4.6	-18.0%	This is a one-time charge for a special project and will not reoccur.
Tech. Support	2.2	17.9%	This is a one-time charge for a special project and will not reoccur.
End User Srvs.	-1.6	-3.0%	This is a one-time charge for a special project and will not reoccur.
Corp. Strategy	3.7	5.5%	This is a one-time charge for a special project and will not reoccur.
Sales/Marketing	0.2	3.2%	This is a one-time charge for a special project and will not reoccur.
Inventory	-1.2	-3.9%	This is a one-time charge for a special project and will not reoccur.
Other	-1	-1000.0%	This is a one-time charge for a special project and will not reoccur.
Totals	-4.8	-2.1%	

Cumulative YTD

Actual ☐ Plan

	VAR-$	VAR-%	Explanation of Variance
Corp. Liaison	-2	-13.3%	This is a one-time charge for a special project and will not reoccur.
Director Staff	-4.3	-21.3%	Temporary hiring primarily for one-time.
Director Staff	0.9	1.8%	This is a one-time charge for a special project and will not reoccur.
Tech. Support	8.4	33.1%	This is a one-time charge for a special project and will not reoccur.
End User Srvs.	4.9	7.2%	This is a one-time charge for a special project and will not reoccur.
Corp. Strategy	14.1	15.6%	This is a one-time charge for a special project and will not reoccur.
Sales/Marketing	0.5	4.9%	This is a one-time charge for a special project and will not reoccur.
Inventory	5	10.8%	This is a one-time charge for a special project and will not reoccur.
Other	-1.1	-91.7%	This is a one-time charge for a special project and will not reoccur.
Totals	26.4	8.1%	

Capital Plan Performance

This monthly report shows actual capital expenditure to plan. Both current period and year-to-date information are shown. Variance to plan for current period and year-to-date are detailed in the lower chart. Included in the information is all capital expenditure for which the IT department has fiduciary responsibility.

A variance summary should be added to the description frame each month. Alternatively, a variance report similar to the IT expense variance by category can be produced if the capital budget is broken down into various categories.

Metrics
◆ Current Period - Actual (Dollars)
◆ Current Period - Plan (Dollars)
◆ Year to Date - Actual (Dollars)
◆ Year to Date - Plan (Dollars)
◆ YTD Variance from Plan - Period (Dollars)
◆ YTD Variance from Plan - YTD (Dollars)

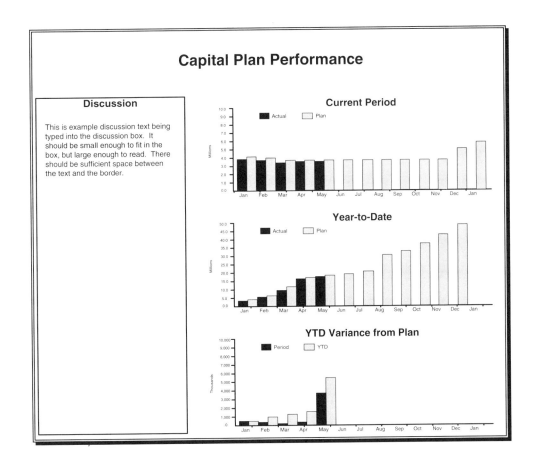

Project Capital Expenditures

We recommend that this report be implemented when the IT department begins budgeting and tracking capital expenditures by project. The report shows the original and the revised capital budget for each project. It also shows the project-to-date and year-to-date expenditures. This report reflects a break down of the overall capital budget performance report discussed earlier. This report is intended for the CIO, the Corporate Executive Committee, and for the project managers in charge of the projects reflected in the report.

The information depicted in this report should be reconciled to the enterprise's fixed asset system. One copy of this report should be prepared for each "major" IT project.

Metrics
◆   Project Capital - Year to Date (Dollars)
◆   Project Capital - Inception to Date (Dollars)
◆   Project Capital - Original Plan (Dollars)
◆   Project Capital - Current Plan (Dollars)
◆   Project Capital - Plan Variance (Dollars)

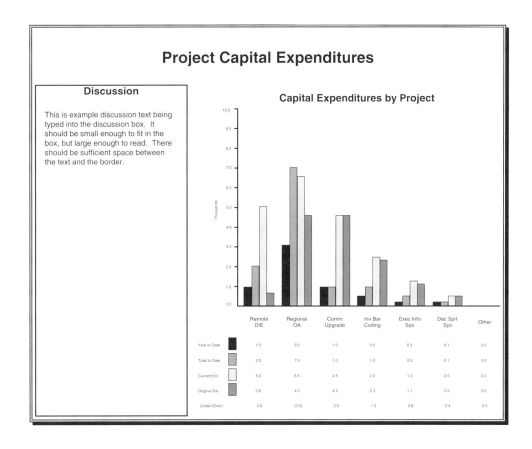

Project Capital Expenditures

Discussion

This is example discussion text being typed into the discussion box. It should be small enough to fit in the box, but large enough to read. There should be sufficient space between the text and the border.

Capital Expenditures by Project

	Remote D/E	Regional OA	Comm Upgrade	Inv Bar Coding	Exec Info Sys	Dec Sprt Sys	Other
Year to Date	1.0	3.0	1.0	0.5	0.3	0.1	0.0
Total to Date	2.0	7.0	1.0	1.0	0.5	0.1	0.0
Current Est.	5.0	6.5	4.5	2.0	1.3	0.5	0.0
Original Est.	0.6	4.5	4.5	2.3	1.1	0.5	0.0
Under/(Over)	3.0	(0.5)	3.5	1.5	0.8	0.4	0.0

Billing Allocation

This is a monthly report reflecting the total IT charges that have been allocated to the markets or other operating units. The report reflects the actual allocations relative to plan. There are very diverse views of the value associated with the process of allocating costs and setting the transfer price between various operating groups. Before this set of metrics is implemented the enterprise should take care to see that all key decision makers agree with the approach selected if it is used.

This report must be integrated with a charge back system. In addition to each individual report, there should be one report that summarizes all billing allocations for the enterprise.

Metrics
◆ Current Period - Actual (Dollars)
◆ Current Period - Plan (Dollars)

Billing Allocation

Discussion

This is example discussion text being typed into the discussion box. It should be small enough to fit in the box, but large enough to read. There should be sufficient space between the text and the border.

Billing Allocation

System Usage by Customer

This report provides a high level summary of usage by market or operating unit. The usage is shown as a percent of total resources used. It is a composite measure developed within the IT department to show the percent of all resources that a particular market or operating unit is consuming in the normal course of business. The report shows both the current period and year-to-date information regarding system usage. In addition because all markets and operating units are shown, it provides an indication of relative usage by each of the units.

This report can be produced from data which is currently available. However, the CIO will need to define the procedures for weighting and consolidating the resource usage data for each IT cost center. This report will accompany the Billing Allocation report.

Metrics
♦ System Usage by Customer - Period (Percent)
♦ System Usage by Customer - YTD (Percent)

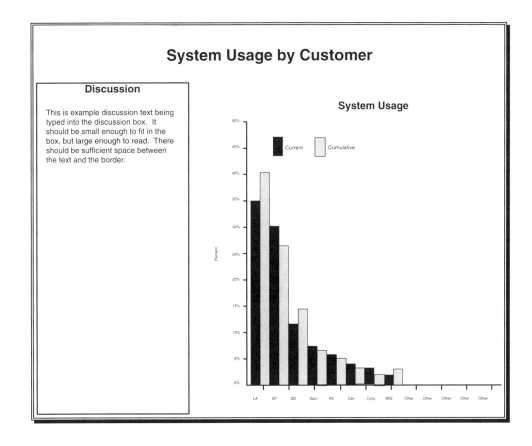

Resource Usage by Customer

The purpose of this report is to show the break down of the IT resource usage for each market or operating unit by the type of resource. A similar report will be prepared for each market or operating unit. Resources can be staff, hardware, capacity of a resource such as bandwidth or time. This will change though time.

This report is intended to support the IT cost allocation or charge back policies and should be included in the SLA reporting package.

This report must be integrated with a charge back system. In addition to each individual report, there should be one report that summaries all usage for the enterprise.

Metrics
◆ Usage by Type - Development (Percent)
◆ Usage by Type - Support (Percent)
◆ Usage by Type - Storage (Percent)
◆ Usage by Type - Processing(Percent)
◆ Usage by Type - Total (Percent)

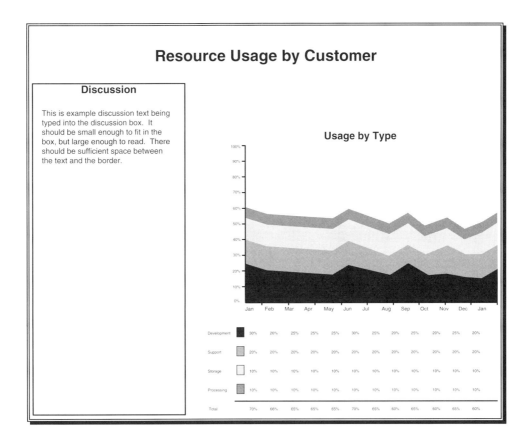

Resource Usage by Customer

Discussion

This is example discussion text being typed into the discussion box. It should be small enough to fit in the box, but large enough to read. There should be sufficient space between the text and the border.

Usage by Type

	Jan	Feb	Mar	Apr	May	Jun	Jul	Aug	Sep	Oct	Nov	Dec	Jan
Development		30%	26%	25%	25%	25%	30%	25%	20%	25%	20%	25%	20%
Support		20%	20%	20%	20%	20%	20%	20%	20%	20%	20%	20%	20%
Storage		10%	10%	10%	10%	10%	10%	10%	10%	10%	10%	10%	10%
Processing		10%	10%	10%	10%	10%	10%	10%	10%	10%	10%	10%	10%
Total		70%	66%	65%	65%	65%	70%	65%	60%	65%	60%	65%	60%

Staff Plan Performance

The purpose of this report is to show a total picture of IT staffing. It shows employee actual head count, planned head count and head count as a percent of plan. It also provides information on contractors including the total number of contractors at the end of the current period as well as the percent of total IT head count that is made up by contractors. This report is intended for the CIO and the Corporate Executive Committee. A similar report would be produced for the directors of the larger IT cost centers.

Metrics

- ◆ Head Count Actual Vs Plan
  - ❐ Actual Employees (FTE)
  - ❐ Actual Contractors (FTE)
  - ❐ Employee Plan (FTE)
- ◆ Staffing Analysis
  - ❐ Actual Employees (FTE)
  - ❐ Actual Contractors (FTE)

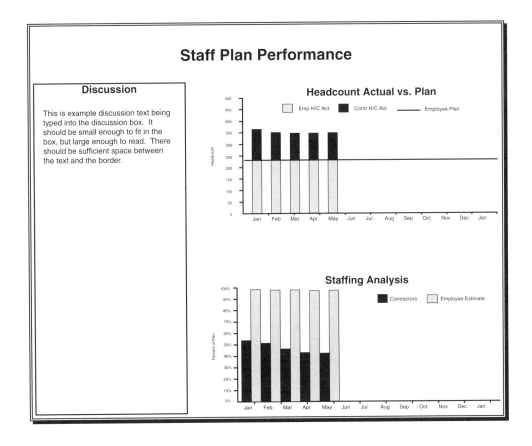

Staff Plan Performance

Discussion

This is example discussion text being typed into the discussion box. It should be small enough to fit in the box, but large enough to read. There should be sufficient space between the text and the border.

Headcount Actual vs. Plan

Emp H/C Act   Contr H/C Act   Employee Plan

Staffing Analysis

Contractors   Employee Estimate

Head Count Summary

This report breaks down the IT head count by cost center and by type of staff. Both contractor and employee information are provided. It shows employee actual head count, planned head count and head count as a percent of plan. It also provides information on contractors including the total number of contractors at the end of the current period as well as the percent of total IT head count that is made up by contractors. This report is intended for the CIO and the Corporate Executive Committee. A similar report would be produced for the directors of the larger IT functions.

Metrics
♦ Employees by Cost Center - Plan (FTE)
♦ Employees by Cost Center - Actual (FTE)
♦ Contractors by Cost Center - Plan (FTE)
♦ Contractors by Cost Center - Actual (FTE)
♦ Total by Cost Center - Actual (FTE)
♦ Total by Cost Center - Plan (FTE)
♦ Total Headcount {by type}- Actual (FTE)
♦ Total Headcount {by type}- Plan (FTE)

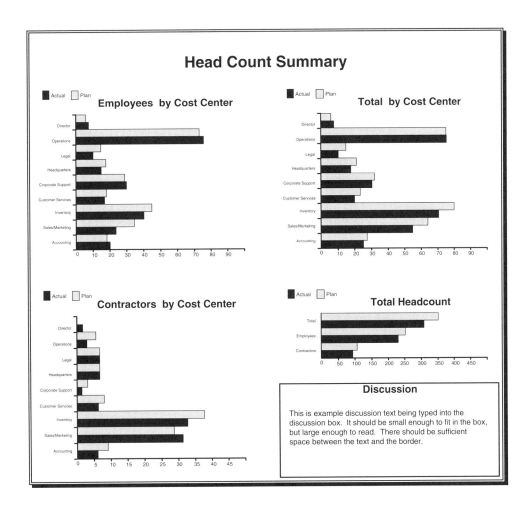

Staff Turnover Report

The report shows the year-to-date turnover by cost center and in total for the IT department. The data on the report shows both actual head count and percentage of total within cost centers. This report is for the use of the CIO and for possible presentation to the Corporate Executive Committee. In addition, the CIO should share this information with his direct reports.

The percent of total can be shown either as the percent of turnover within a given cost center or it can be shown as a percent of total IT department turnover. This should be determined when the report is put into production.

A similar report would be produced for the directors of the larger IT functions.

Metrics

- ♦ YTD Staff Turnover by Department (Percent)
- ♦ YTD Staff Turnover by Department (Count)

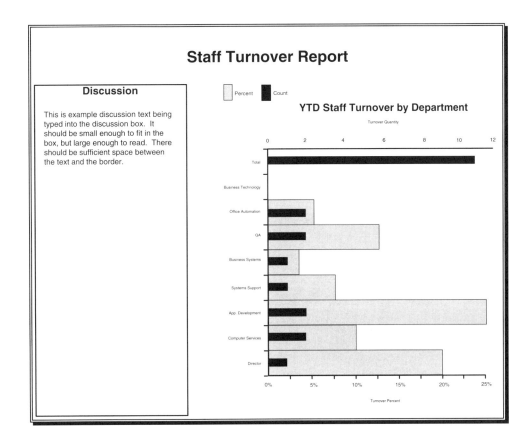

Protected Classes Summary

This report breaks down the IT protected class head counts by cost center and by type of staff. It shows employee actual head count, planned head count and head count as a percent of plan. It also provides information on protected classes including the total number of protected class individuals at the end of the current period as well as the percent of total IT head count that is made up by protected classes. This report is intended for the CIO and the Corporate Executive Committee. A similar report would be produced for the directors of the larger IT functions.

Metrics

♦ Number of Minorities (Single Class) Employees

♦ Number of Minorities (Multiple Classes) Employees

♦ Number of ADA Employees

♦ Total Number of Employees

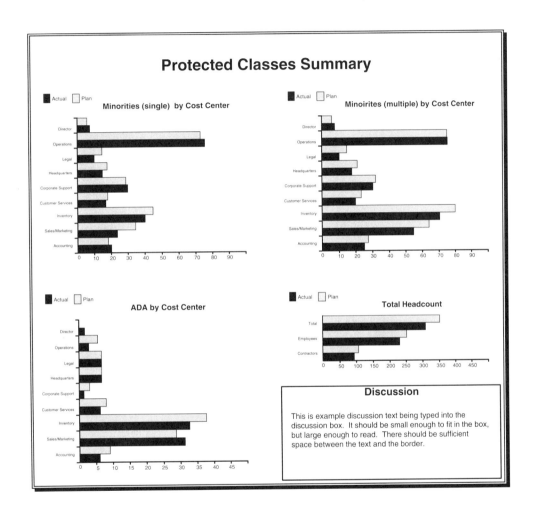

User Penetration Count

The report shows the penetration of Internet (or Intranet) within the enterprise by the number of users. The data on the report shows both actual number of users and percentage of total within the enterprise (or department). This report is for the use of the CIO and for possible presentation to the Corporate Executive Committee. In addition, the CIO should share this information with his direct reports.

A similar report would be produced for the directors of the larger IT functions.

Metrics

- ◆ Number of Total Users (Plan/Actual)
- ◆ Number of Total User Hours (Plan/Actual)
- ◆ Number Users by Department(Plan/Actual)
- ◆ Number User Hours by Department (Plan/Actual)
- ◆ Cost of External Internet Services (Pop Accounts)
- ◆ Cost of External Internet Products (i.e. Databases)
- ◆ FTP Volume (Plan/Actual)
- ◆ Telnet Volume (Plan/Actual)
- ◆ Top Ten Users (Size/Count)
- ◆ Non-Users - Inactive Users

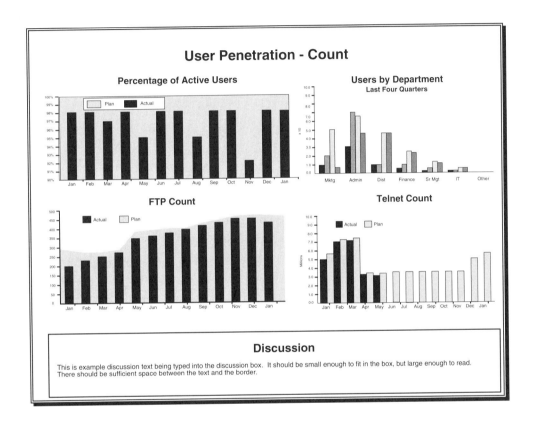

User Penetration Volume

The report shows the penetration of Internet (or Intranet) within the enterprise by the amount of usage. The data on the report shows actual hours and volume within the enterprise (or department). This report is for the use of the CIO and for possible presentation to the Corporate Executive Committee. In addition, the CIO should share this information with his direct reports.

A similar report would be produced for the directors of the larger IT functions.

Metrics

- ◆ Number of Total Users (Plan/Actual)
- ◆ Number of Total User Hours (Plan/Actual)
- ◆ Number Users by Department(Plan/Actual)
- ◆ Number User Hours by Department (Plan/Actual)
- ◆ Cost of External Internet Services (Pop Accounts)
- ◆ Cost of External Internet Products (i.e. Databases)
- ◆ FTP Volume (Plan/Actual)
- ◆ Telnet Volume (Plan/Actual)
- ◆ Top Ten Users (Size/Count)
- ◆ Non-Users - Inactive Users

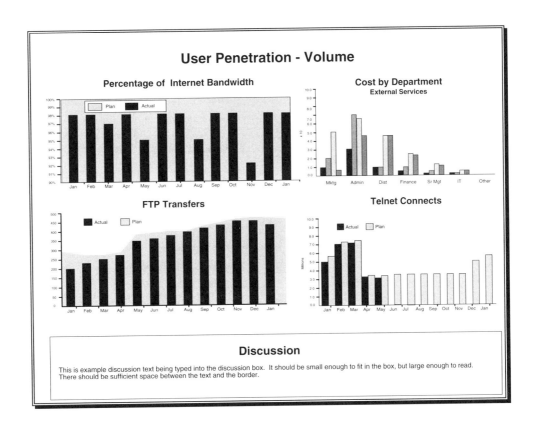

E-mail Traffic

The report shows the penetration of E-Mail within the enterprise by the number and amount of usage. The data on the report shows actual volume within the enterprise (or department). This report is for the use of the CIO and for possible presentation to the Corporate Executive Committee. In addition, the CIO should share this information with his direct reports.

A similar report would be produced for the directors of the larger IT functions.

Metrics
◆ Internal E-Mail Users (Plan/Actual)
◆ Internal E-Mail Messages (Plan/Actual)
◆ Inbound External E-Mail Messages/Size
◆ Outbound External E-Mail Messages/Size
◆ Electronic Post Office Size
◆ Top Ten Users (Size/Count/In/Out)
◆ Inactive Users
◆ Top Ten Oldest Messages Not Opened

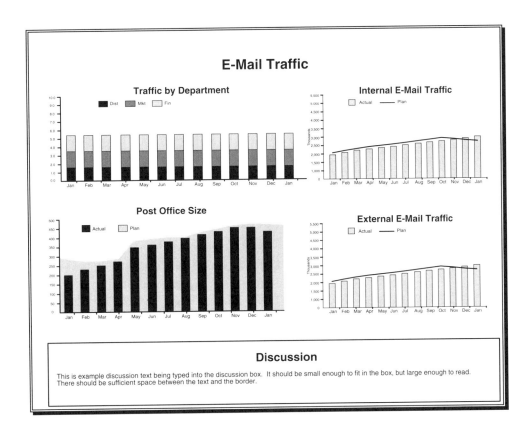

USENET Traffic

The report shows the penetration and usage of USENET mail groups within the enterprise by the number and amount of usage. The data on the report shows actual volume within the enterprise (or department). This report is for the use of the CIO and for possible presentation to the Corporate Executive Committee. In addition, the CIO should share this information with his direct reports.

A similar report would be produced for the directors of the larger IT functions.

Metrics
♦ USENET User Counts (Plan/Actual)
♦ USENET User Hours (Plan/Actual)
♦ USENET Transfer Volume (Plan/Actual)
♦ USENET Files Size (Plan/Actual)
♦ USENET Posting Size (Plan/Actual)
♦ USENET Positing Number (Plan/Actual)
♦ Largest Thread Size - Enterprise Newsgroups
♦ Postings by Number - Enterprise Newsgroups

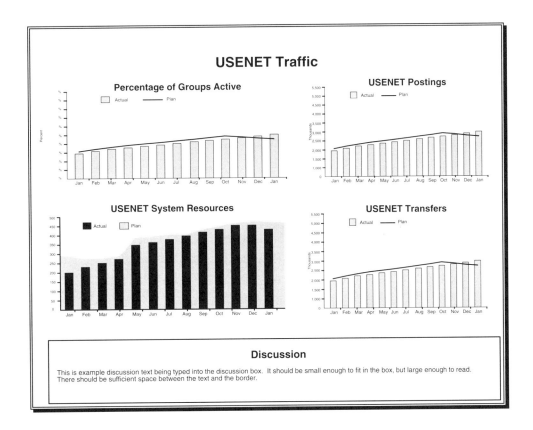

USENET Traffic

Percentage of Groups Active

USENET Postings

USENET System Resources

USENET Transfers

Discussion

This is example discussion text being typed into the discussion box. It should be small enough to fit in the box, but large enough to read. There should be sufficient space between the text and the border.

WEB Statistics

The report shows volume statistics within the enterprise by the number and amount of "hits" on particular WEB pages. The data on the report shows actual volume within the enterprise (or department). This report is for the use of the CIO and for possible presentation to the Corporate Executive Committee. In addition, the CIO should share this information with his direct reports.

A similar report would be produced for the directors of the larger IT functions.

Metrics
♦ Number of Hits (Plan/Actual)
♦ Top Ten WEB Pages
♦ Number of Direct Inquiries To Enterprise
♦ Number of WEB Page Changes
♦ Bottom Ten WEB Pages
♦ WEB Page Aging
♦ WEB Hits By Hour

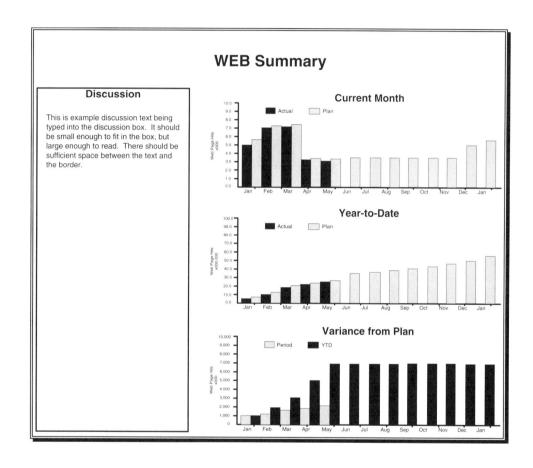

WEB Summary

Discussion

This is example discussion text being typed into the discussion box. It should be small enough to fit in the box, but large enough to read. There should be sufficient space between the text and the border.

Current Month

Year-to-Date

Variance from Plan

Electronic Commerce Sales

The report shows volume and dollar statistics for sales activity within the enterprise by the number and amount of electronic transactions. The data on the report shows actual volume within the enterprise (or department). This report is for the use of the CIO and for possible presentation to the Corporate Executive Committee. In addition, the CIO should share this information with his direct reports.

A similar report would be produced for the directors of the larger IT functions.

Metrics
◆ Product Inquiries Via Internet
◆ Sales - Number of Orders (Plan/Actual)
◆ Sales - Dollar Volume Orders (Plan/Actual)
◆ Sales by Product Offering

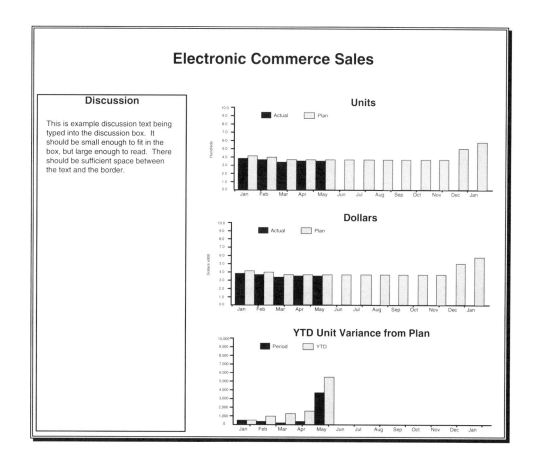

Electronic Commerce Returns

The report shows volume and dollar statistics for return activity within the enterprise by the number and amount of electronic transactions. The data on the report shows actual volume within the enterprise (or department). This report is for the use of the CIO and for possible presentation to the Corporate Executive Committee. In addition, the CIO should share this information with his direct reports.

A similar report would be produced for the directors of the larger IT functions.

Metrics

- ◆ Return Orders - Number (Plan/Actual)
- ◆ Return Orders - Dollars (Plan/Actual)
- ◆ Returns by Product

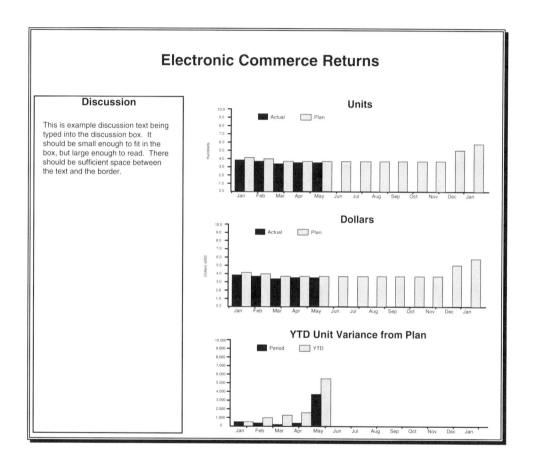

High Volume Users

The report shows the high volume users of the system. This report is for the use of the CIO and for possible presentation to the Corporate Executive Committee. In addition, the CIO should share this information with his direct reports and key managers to whom these high volume users report.

A similar report would be produced for the directors of the larger IT functions.

Metrics
◆ High Volume E-mail (Inbound/Outbound)
◆ High Volume FTP
◆ High Volume Telnet
◆ High Volume USENET Postings (Internet/Internet)

High Volume Users

E-mail

Name	Location	Count
Lang, Richard	Chicago	578 Messages
Janulaitis, Victor	Boston	432
Wilson, Angela	Los Angeles	400
Baskerville, Tom	London	356
Isip, Jay	Detriot	356
Perkins, Arnie	Dallas	352
Laskey, Bob	Los Angeles	300
Huff, Shalon	Los Angeles	295

FTP

Name	Location	Count
Geroge, Richard	Chicago	578 K Xfered
Janulaitis, Victor	Boston	432 K
Wilson, Dave	Los Angeles	400 K
Baskerville, Tom	London	356 K
Knapp, Elsa	Detriot	356 K
Perkins, Arnie	Dallas	352 K
Laskey, Bob	Los Angeles	300 K
Huff, Shalon	Los Angeles	295 K

Telnet

Name	Location	Count
Squiers, Mark	Chicago	578 Connections
Janulaitis, Victor	Boston	432
Jones, Dave	Los Angeles	400
Baskerville, Tom	London	356
Gerorge, Ron	Detriot	356
Perkins, Arnie	Dallas	352
Laskey, Bob	Los Angeles	300
Huff, Shalon	Los Angeles	295

USENET

Name	Location	Count
Wilson, Larry	Chicago	578 Postings
Janulaitis, Victor	Boston	432
Wilson, Susan	Los Angeles	400
Baskerville, Tom	London	356
Hunt, Jay	Detriot	356
Perkins, Arnie	Dallas	352
Laskey, Bob	Los Angeles	300
Huff, Shalon	Los Angeles	295

Discussion

This is example discussion text being typed into the discussion box. It should be small enough to fit in the box, but large enough to read. There should be sufficient space between the text and the border.

Low Volume Users

The report shows the low volume users of the system. This report is for the use of the CIO and for possible presentation to the Corporate Executive Committee. In addition, the CIO should share this information with his direct reports and key managers to whom these low volume users report.

A similar report would be produced for the directors of the larger IT functions.

Metrics
◆ Low Volume E-mail (Inbound/Outbound)
◆ Low Volume FTP
◆ Low Volume Telnet
◆ Low Volume USENET Postings (Internet/Internet)

Low Volume Users

E-mail

Name	Location	Count
George, Richard	Chicago	0 Messages
Janulaitis, Victor	Boston	0
Wilson, Angela	Los Angeles	0
Baskerville, Carol	London	1
Isip, Jay	Detriot	1
Perkins, Arnie	Dallas	2
Lang, Richard	Los Angeles	2
Huff, Shalon	Los Angeles	2

FTP

Name	Location	Count
Wilson, Larry	Chicago	0 K Xfered
Janulaitis, Victor	Boston	0 K
Wilson, Dave	Los Angeles	0 K
Baskerville, Tom	London	0 K
Isip, Victoria	Detriot	0 K
Perkins, Arnie	Dallas	0 K
Laskey, Bob	Los Angeles	0 K
Huff, Shalon	Los Angeles	0 K

Telnet

Name	Location	Count
Squires, Peggy	Chicago	0 Connedtions
Janulaitis, Victor	Boston	0
Wilson, Dave	Los Angeles	0
Baskerville, Tom	London	0
Tepper, Matthew	Detriot	0
Perkins, Arnie	Dallas	0
Laskey, Bob	Los Angeles	0
Huff, Shalon	Los Angeles	0

USENET

Name	Location	Count
Able, Mary	Chicago	0 Postings
Janulaitis, Victor	Boston	0
Geroge, Ron	Los Angeles	1
Baskerville, Tom	London	2
Isip, Jay	Detriot	3
Perkins, Vyda	Dallas	4
Laskey, Bob	Los Angeles	5
Huff, Shalon	Los Angeles	6

Discussion

This is example discussion text being typed into the discussion box. It should be small enough to fit in the box, but large enough to read. There should be sufficient space between the text and the border.

Revenue & Capital

The report compares revenue and capital expenditures to that of the enterprise as a whole. Three measures are presented on the report: (1) expenses as a percent of enterprise revenues; (2) expenses as a dollar amount per active customer; and (3) capital employed at current book value as a percent of enterprise revenues for the past twelve months. This report is for the CIO and provides relevant information for comparing the enterprise's operations to others in the industry.

The first and last of these measures are used in the calculations of annual industry surveys. For the first measure, the expense and revenue are actual period values. If the data fluctuates widely, a smoothing approach should be adopted such as a three month moving average. For the last measure, capital is calculated at current book value and enterprise revenues are the total revenue for the previous twelve months of operations. (Note: in a number of industry surveys related to this measure, the capital value is based on the resale value of computer processors only not book value).

Metrics
♦ Expense as Percent of Revenue - Plan (Ratio)
♦ Expense as Percent of Revenue - Actual (Ratio)
♦ Expense per Customer - Plan (Dollars)[41]
♦ Expense per Customer - Actual (Dollars)
♦ Capital as Percent of Revenue Plan (Percent)
♦ Capital as Percent of Revenue Actual (Percent)

---

[41] In the case of a company that has 30,000 customers, cost would be Expense per Customer. Some enterprises will use a measure associated with the service provided. In the airline industry a measure used is Cost per Revenue Passenger Mile.

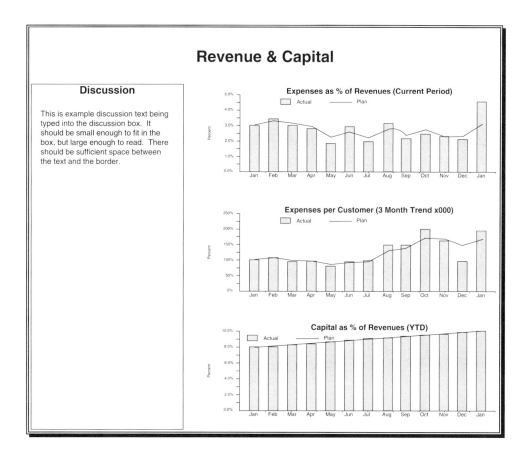

Revenue & Capital

Discussion

This is example discussion text being typed into the discussion box. It should be small enough to fit in the box, but large enough to read. There should be sufficient space between the text and the border.

Expenses as % of Revenues (Current Period)

Actual · Plan

Expenses per Customer (3 Month Trend x000)

Actual · Plan

Capital as % of Revenues (YTD)

Actual · Plan

Expenses & Staffing

The purpose of this report is to compare expense and head count to equivalent enterprise data. There are three measures on the report: (1) IT to enterprise expenses; (2) to enterprise staffing; and (3) a hybrid of the first two measures showing the cost per corporate head count. This report is for the CIO and for presentation to the Corporate Executive Committee. On all three measures a three month moving average trend is shown on the report along with the actual ratio.

As an alternative metric to cost per employee the reader might consider cost per customer or cost per product or some other relevant business measure.

Metrics

- ◆ IT vs. Company Expense 3 Month Trend
  - ❐ Plan (Percent)
  - ❐ Actual (Percent)
- ◆ IT vs. Company Staffing 3 Month Trend
  - ❐ Plan (Percent)
  - ❐ Actual (Percent)
- ◆ IT Cost per Company Employee 3 Month Trend
  - ❐ Plan (Dollars)
  - ❐ Actual (Dollars)

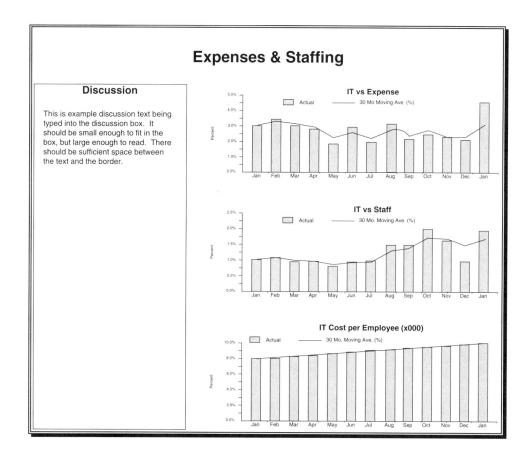

Competitive Application Matrix

The purpose of this report is to identify applications is use by direct competitors to the enterprise. This report is for the CIO and for presentation to the Corporate Executive Committee. On all three measures a three month moving average trend is shown on the report along with the actual ratio. There are many ways to present this information but the key is to keep it as simple as possible while providing meaningful information that non IT professionals can assimilate.

Information of this nature is normally difficult to capture, however there are sources that can be easily tapped:

> ❐ Industry Associations
>
> ❐ Ex-employees
>
> ❐ Vendors
>
> ❐ Trade Press (least reliable)

Metrics

> ◆ Key Industry Applications
> > ❐ Enterprise Status and Staffing
> > ❐ Competitor Status and Staffing
> ◆ Technologies Used
> > ❐ Enterprise
> > ❐ Competitors
> ◆ IT Metrics
> > ❐ Enterprise Focus
> > ❐ Competitors Focus

Competitive Application Martix

	Enterprise	Competitor A	Competitor B	Competitor C
Revenues Size Ops	$100MM 200 Units	$200MM 2,000 Units	$175MM 800 Units	$2,000MM 3,000 Units
IT Size	52 IT $53MM	100-125 IT $89MM	125-155 IT $99MM	500-525 IT $189MM
Order Entry	9 years old IBM/Cobol	1 year old Visual C	Implementing Sybase (In process)	Outsourcing now
Marketing	3 years old IBM/Cobol	6 months old Client Server	Implementing Sybase (In process)	Implementing Sybase (In process)
Field Ops	3 years old IBM/Cobol	Outsourced	3 years old IBM/Cobol	1 year old Visual C
Manufacturing	9 years old IBM/Cobol	3 years old IBM/Cobol	1 year old Visual C	1 year old Visual C
Distrbution	9 years old IBM/Cobol	Implementing Sybase (In process)	Implementing Sybase (In process)	3 years old IBM/Cobol

Discussion

This is example discussion text being typed into the discussion box. It should be small enough to fit in the box, but large enough to read. There should be sufficient space between the text and the border.

Technology Penetration Trends

The purpose of this report is to show the extent to which IT workstations have been introduced to the organization. Information is provided on the use of personal computers, standard computer terminals, and in total. This information is intended for the CIO and his presentation to the Corporate Executive Committee.

The information in this report is used in the calculation of the comparisons to annual industry survey statistics. Where possible, this report should be produced as a comparative report to an enterprise's primary and secondary competitors.

In many enterprises this report may be produced once a year instead of quarterly. In many enterprises, quarterly reporting may be overkill.

Metrics

- ◆ Devices vs. Employees (Number)

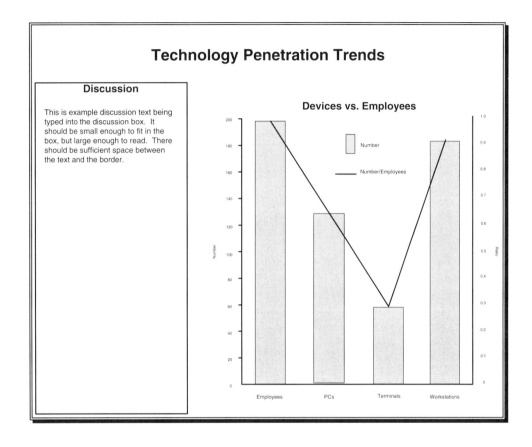

Technology Penetration Trends

Discussion

This is example discussion text being typed into the discussion box. It should be small enough to fit in the box, but large enough to read. There should be sufficient space between the text and the border.

Devices vs. Employees

Number

Number/Employees

Development Productivity

The purpose of this report is to show current period productivity and overall productivity improvement trends within the IT application development staff. This report is intended for the CIO, the director in charge of applications development and possibly for presentation to the Executive Committee.

There are two prerequisites for implementing productivity reporting. First, the IT organization must adopt systems development methodologies that lead to the measurement of work. One of the more common is function point.

Development and maintenance efforts must be separate from one another. Units of work can be lines of code produced or lines of code modified or can be function points produced. Second, the IT department needs to have a formal time keeping system whereby hours can be tracked by project task.

Metrics
◆ Units of Work[42] - Plan (Count)
◆ Units of Work - Actual (Count)
◆ Development Staffing - Headcount (Actual)
◆ Development Staffing - Headcount (FTE)
◆ Development Productivity Ratio
❐ Units of Work per FTE
❐ Units of Work per Actual
❐ Units of Work Target

---

[42] Units of work can be items such as function points. Better measures are a number of events completed by the group such as number of modules moved into production for a development organization or number of phone calls answered by a customer services organization.

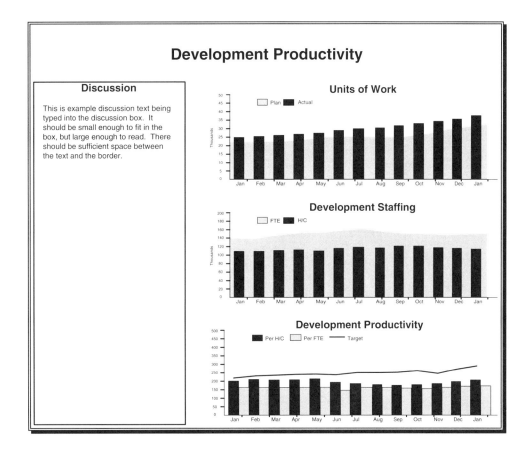

Development Productivity

Discussion

This is example discussion text being typed into the discussion box. It should be small enough to fit in the box, but large enough to read. There should be sufficient space between the text and the border.

Units of Work

Development Staffing

Development Productivity

Production Support Productivity

This report shows productivity of the operations support staff. The unit of work for this report can be number of jobs processed in a batch environment or number of on-line transactions processed. The input is the number of production support or technical support hours that are required to keep the processing resources in an operational state. This report is for the CIO, the Operations Director, and possibly for presentation to the Corporate Executive Committee.

As an alternative metric to this the reader might consider number of customer inquiries (or changes) or products manufactured or sold or some other relevant business measure.

Metrics

- ♦ Job Processed Plan (Count)
- ♦ Jobs Processed Actual (Count)
- ♦ Support Staffing - Headcount (Actual)
- ♦ Support Staffing - Headcount (FTE)
- ♦ Production Productivity Ratio
  - ❑ Jobs Processed per FTE
  - ❑ Jobs Processed per Actual
  - ❑ Jobs Processed Target

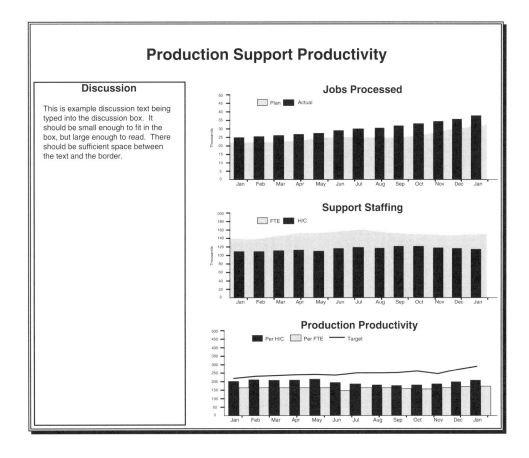

Production Support Productivity

Discussion

This is example discussion text being typed into the discussion box. It should be small enough to fit in the box, but large enough to read. There should be sufficient space between the text and the border.

Jobs Processed

Plan Actual

Support Staffing

FTE H/C

Production Productivity

Per H/C Per FTE Target

Response Time Report - Report A

Many metrics on response time are internal to the IT function and are not correlated to the user's vision of performance. This set of metrics is intended to be a measure of the service that is received by the user over the period of a week.

This type of report is intended to show overall response time of a particular user related function on a day-to-day basis. Similar metrics comparing day of week by week or month can be produced. This report should be included in the SLA report package.

Note: This report was produced using Positive Support Review's performance monitor -- UVP. Please see section discussing UVP.

Metrics
◆   Application User Response Time

Response Time Report A

Discussion

This is example discussion text being typed into the discussion box. It should be small enough to fit in the box, but large enough to read. There should be sufficient space between the text and the border.

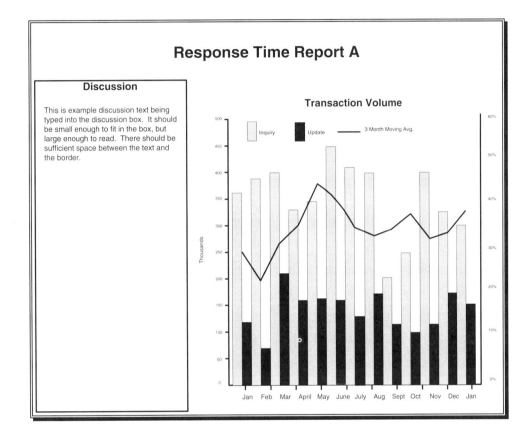

Response Time Report - Report B

Many metrics on response time are internal to the IT function and are not correlated to the user's vision of performance. This set of metrics is intended to be a measure of the service that is received by the user over a normal work day.

This type of report is intended to show overall response time of a particular user related function on a day-to-day basis. Similar metrics comparing day of week by week or month can be produced. This report should be included in the SLA report package.

Note: This report was produced using Positive Support Review's performance monitor -- UVP. Please see section discussing UVP.

Metrics

♦   Application User Response Time

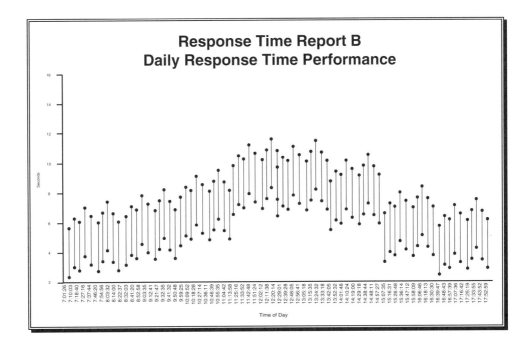

Service Request Backlog

This report shows the backlog of service requests for the IT application development group. There are three measures on the report. The first measure shows the number of service requests outstanding and the number that have been submitted and closed each period. The second measure shows the same information but in level of effort (i.e., number of hours). This report shows the backlog and the level of effort submitted and completed. It also shows the current capacity of the development department to satisfy these requests. The third measure shows the average time to complete the different priority service requests. This report is intended for the CIO, the director of applications development, and for the Executive Committee. In addition, a version of this report should be produced for each market or operating unit which reflects only the system requests relevant to that business unit. This later version of the report should be included in the SLA reporting package.

Metrics

- ◆ Number of Service Requests - Opened (Count)
- ◆ Number of Service Requests - Closed (Count)
- ◆ Number of Service Requests - Backlog (Count)
- ◆ Backlog - Actual (Number Days)
- ◆ Backlog - Plan (Number Days)
- ◆ Time to Complete Priority 1 (Days)
- ◆ Time to Complete Priority 2 (Days)
- ◆ Time to Complete Priority 3 (Days)

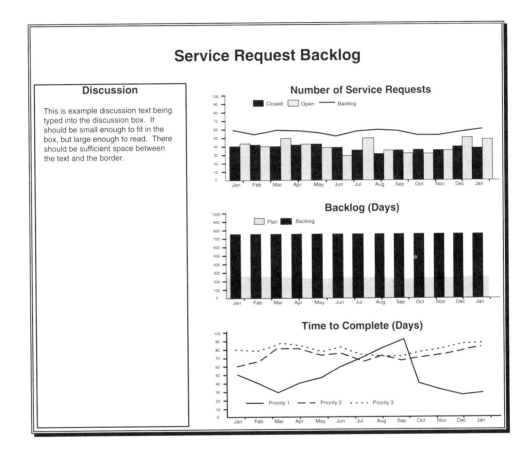

Project Status Report

This report provides a one page summary of the significant projects within IT. The project report can be used for application development, for hardware implementation, or office automation projects. The report is intended for the CIO, the Project Managers in charge of each significant project, the Executive Committee, and for inclusion in the SLA reporting package for each affected business unit.

Much has been written on project management. The one lesson we have learned is the value of a single page report that summarizes time, cost and staffing.

Metrics

- ♦ Detail Budget and Status by Step[43]
    - ❒ Man Hours Approved
    - ❒ Man Hours Actual
    - ❒ Man Hours Estimated to Complete
    - ❒ Man Hours Total to Complete
    - ❒ Man Hours Variance

---

43   Steps for many projects are defined by a company's System Development Methodology (SDM)

Project Status Report

Discussion

This is example discussion text being typed into the discussion box. It should be small enough to fit in the box, but large enough to read. There should be sufficient space between the text and the border.

Detail Budget and Schedule Status

	Jan 1	Feb 1	Mar 1	Apr 1	May 1	Jun 1
Project Planning - Plan						
Actual						
Req. Definition - Plan						
Actual						
External Design - Plan						
Actual						
Internal Design - Plan						
Actual						
Prog. & Unit Test - Plan						
Actual						
System Testing - Plan						
Actual						
Impl. & Training - Plan						
Actual						
Conversion - Plan						
Actual						

	Approved Man Hours	Actual Man Hours	Comp. Est. Man Hours	Total Man Hours	Variance Man Hours	%
Project to Date	133	70	0	70	63	47%

Service Request Aging

This report provides a one page summary of the age of all service requests within IT. The report can be used to communicate the number and age of all maintenance work within IT. The report is intended for the CIO, the Project Managers in charge of each major system and function within IT, the Executive Committee, and for inclusion in the SLA reporting package for each affected business unit.

Metrics

♦   Aged Service Requests by Type

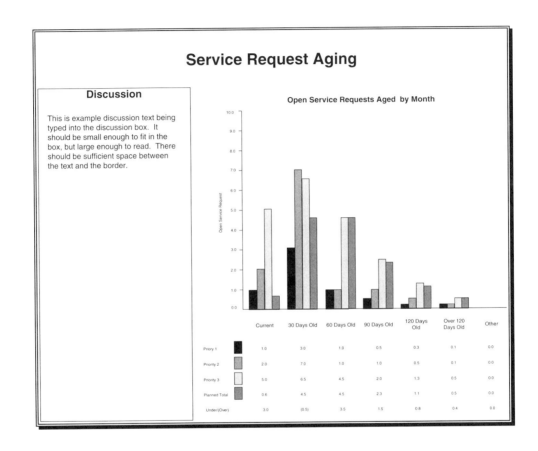

Service Request Aging

Discussion

This is example discussion text being typed into the discussion box. It should be small enough to fit in the box, but large enough to read. There should be sufficient space between the text and the border.

Open Service Requests Aged by Month

	Current	30 Days Old	60 Days Old	90 Days Old	120 Days Old	Over 120 Days Old	Other
Priory 1	1.0	3.0	1.0	0.5	0.3	0.1	0.0
Priority 2	2.0	7.0	1.0	1.0	0.5	0.1	0.0
Priority 3	5.0	6.5	4.5	2.0	1.3	0.5	0.0
Planned Total	0.6	4.5	4.5	2.3	1.1	0.5	0.0
Under/(Over)	3.0	(0.5)	3.5	1.5	0.8	0.4	0.0

Service Request Closure Priority 1

This report provides service level reporting regarding the on-time completion of priority one service requests (SR). For priority one SRs, a typical performance goal is that ninety percent of the SRs be completed by the original scheduled completion date. This report will be produced for all SRs completed in a given month. It will also be produced for each market or business unit. The primary audience for this report is the CIO, the director in charge of application development, and the market representatives.

Services requests for purpose of this book are defined:
Priority 1 - Must fix now, system will not run
Priority 2 -- Need to fix soon, user has a work around
Priority 3 -- Enhancement to the system

Metrics
♦ Priority 1 Service Requests Closed - Actual (Count)
♦ Priority 1 Service Requests Closed - Plan (Count)

Service Request Closure Priority 1

Discussion

This is example discussion text being typed into the discussion box. It should be small enough to fit in the box, but large enough to read. There should be sufficient space between the text and the border.

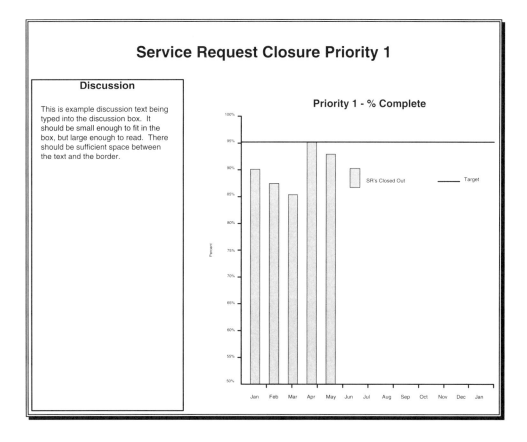

Priority 1 - % Complete

SR's Closed Out   Target

Service Request Closure Priority 2 and 3

This report provides service level reporting regarding the on-time completion of priority two and three service requests (SR). For both priority two and three SRs, a typical performance goal is that ninety percent of the SRs be completed by the original scheduled completion date. This report will be produced for all SRs completed in a given month. It will also be produced for each market or business unit. The primary audience for this report is the CIO, the director in charge of application development, and the market representatives.

Services requests for purpose of this book are defined:
Priority 1 -- Must fix now, system will not run
Priority 2 -- Need to fix soon, user has a work around
Priority 3 -- Enhancement to the system

Metrics
◆ Priority 2 Service Requests Closed - Actual (Count)
◆ Priority 2 Service Requests Closed - Plan (Count)
◆ Priority 3 Service Requests Closed - Actual (Count)
◆ Priority 3 Service Requests Closed - Plan (Count)

Service Request Closure Priority 2 and 3

Discussion

This is example discussion text being typed into the discussion box. It should be small enough to fit in the box, but large enough to read. There should be sufficient space between the text and the border.

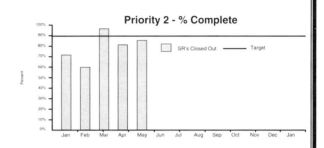

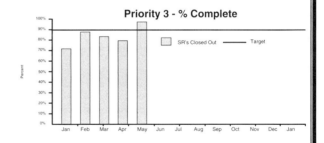

Conversion Status

This report provides conversion reporting regarding the status of a conversion and the quality of the data. The primary audience for this report is the using organization. The secondary audience is the CIO, the director in charge of application development, and the market representatives.

This a report that should be canceled after all of the data is converted to the new system.

Metrics
◆ Number Records (Value)
◆ Number Records Converted (Value)
◆ Conversion - records in error (Value)
◆ Conversion - projected error records (Value)

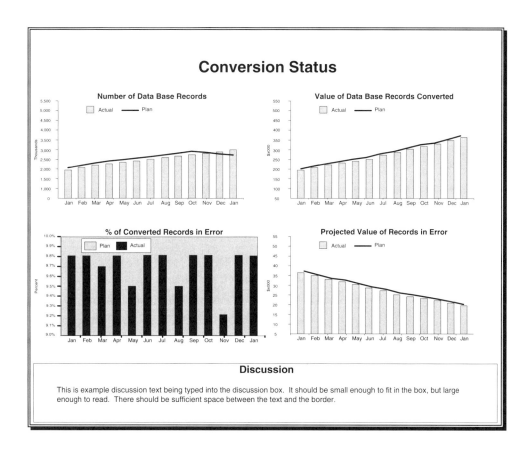

Reengineered Service Performance

This report shows the level of work and the cost per work order for the service requests handled by the administrative support function. There are three measures on the report. The first measure is the number of service work orders that are processed in a given month. The second measure is the cost of service, which includes contract costs allocated across all months of the contract period plus specific charges for out of scope work performed during the reporting period. The third measure shows the cost per work order. The report will be distributed to the CIO and to the director of the function. This report can be applied to any function that goes through a reengineering process or downsizes.

Metrics
◆ Number Service Work Orders - Plan (Count)
◆ Number Service Work Orders - Actual (Count)
◆ Cost of Service - Plan (Dollars)
◆ Cost of Service - Actual (Dollars)
◆ Cost per Service Order- Plan (Dollars per)
◆ Cost per Service Order- Actual (Dollars per)

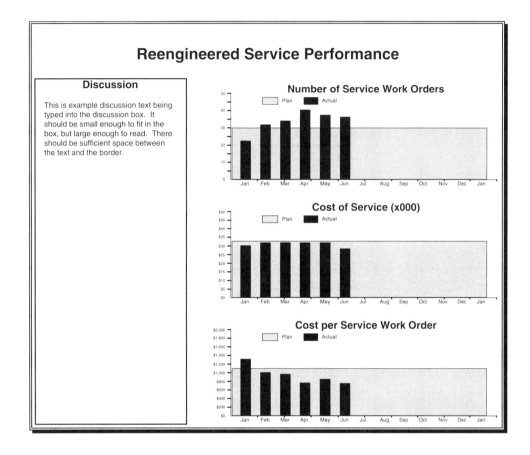

Home Office Workers

This report provides a one page summary of the extent of Home Office Work and the impact on the IT function. The report is intended for the CIO, the key operating group mangers, the Executive Committee, and for inclusion in the monthly operational reporting package for each affected business unit.

Metrics
◆ Number of Home Office Worker Hours (FTEs) (Plan/Actual)
◆ Number of Home Office E-Mail Messages
◆ Number of Home Office Faxes Sent/Received
◆ Hours of Paid In Office Parking
◆ Miles Home Office Workers Reimbursed

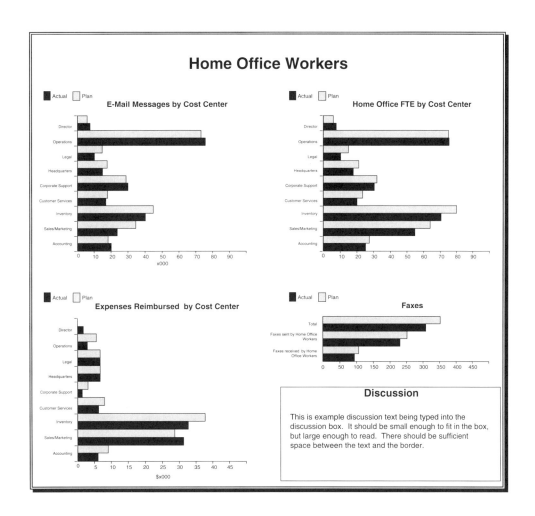

Home Office Productivity

This report provides a one page summary of the productivity of home office workers versus in office workers. The report is intended for the CIO, the key operating group mangers, the Executive Committee, and for inclusion in the monthly operational reporting package for each affected business unit.

Metrics
♦ Number of Home Office Work Hours vs. Number of Total Work Hours
♦ Number of Home Office E-Mail Messages vs. Number of in Office E-Mail Messages
♦ Number of Home Office Faxes Sent/Received vs. Number of in Offices Faxes Sent/Received

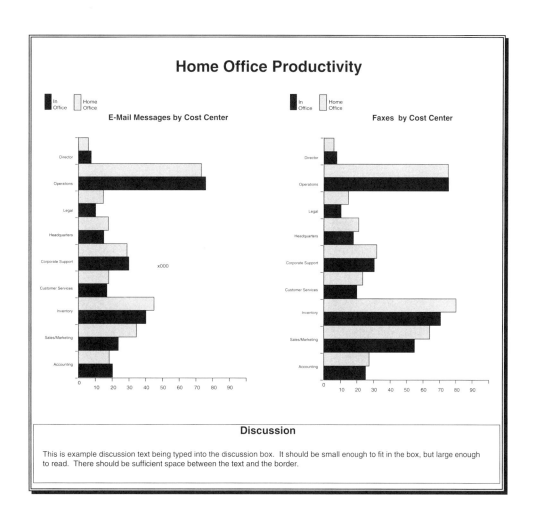

Home Office Productivity

E-Mail Messages by Cost Center

Faxes by Cost Center

Discussion

This is example discussion text being typed into the discussion box. It should be small enough to fit in the box, but large enough to read. There should be sufficient space between the text and the border.

E-Mail Usage

This report provides a one page summary of the significant projects within IT. The project report can be used for application development, for hardware implementation, or office automation projects. The report is intended for the CIO, the Project Managers in charge of each significant project, the Executive Committee, and for inclusion in the SLA reporting package for each affected business unit.

Metrics

♦ Number of Inbound Messages

♦ Number of Outbound Messages

♦ Percentage of Disk Full (Percent)

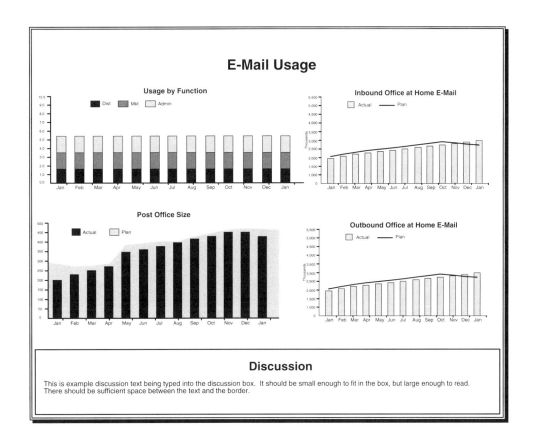

Voice Mail Usage

This report provides a one page summary of the significant projects within IT. The project report can be used for application development, for hardware implementation, or office automation projects. The report is intended for the CIO, the Project Managers in charge of each significant project, the Executive Committee, and for inclusion in the SLA reporting package for each affected business unit.

Metrics
♦ Number of Users Plan
♦ Number of Users Actual
♦ Percentage of Disk Full (Percent)

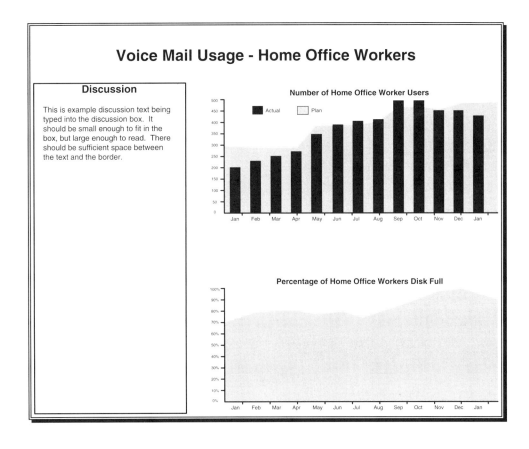

Voice Mail Usage - Home Office Workers

Discussion

This is example discussion text being typed into the discussion box. It should be small enough to fit in the box, but large enough to read. There should be sufficient space between the text and the border.

Number of Home Office Worker Users

■ Actual   □ Plan

Percentage of Home Office Workers Disk Full

215

Project Status Report - Reengineering

This report provides a one page summary of the significant projects within IT. The project report can be used for application development, for hardware implementation, or office automation projects. The report is intended for the CIO, the Project Managers in charge of each significant project, the Executive Committee, and for inclusion in the SLA reporting package for each affected business unit.

Much has been written on project management. The one lesson we have learned is the value of a single page report that summarizes time, cost and staffing.

Metrics

- ◆ Detail Budget and Status by Step[44]
  - ❏ Man Hours Approved
  - ❏ Man Hours Actual
  - ❏ Man Hours Estimated to Complete
  - ❏ Man Hours Total to Complete
  - ❏ Man Hours Variance

---

44   Steps for many projects are defined by a company's System Development Methodology (SDM)

Project Status Report - Reengineering

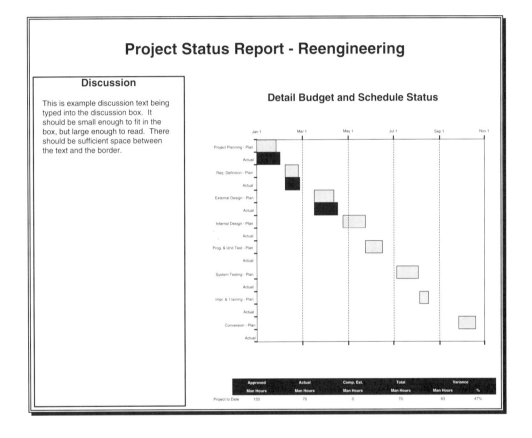

Test Results by Release

This daily report shows the problems identified during pre-release of an application. A similar report will be produced for testing each major release of that application. The report shows the number of problems reported each day and the number of problems resolved each day. Problems are broken down by priority. Cumulative problems outstanding at the end of the reporting period are shown in the third report. In addition a break down of the outstanding problems by priority is provided. The report is distributed to the director of Quality Assurance and to the CIO.

A special report will be prepared following each application release, which compares the number of problems identified during pre-release testing and the level of testing effort expended.

Metrics

- ◆ Number of Problems Reported
  - ❒ Priority 1 (Count)
  - ❒ Priority 2 (Count)
  - ❒ Priority 3 (Count)
- ◆ Number of Problems Resolved
  - ❒ Priority 1 (Count)
  - ❒ Priority 2 (Count)
  - ❒ Priority 3 (Count)
- ◆ Number of Problems Outstanding
  - ❒ Priority 1 (Count)
  - ❒ Priority 2 (Count)
  - ❒ Priority 3 (Count)

Test Results by Release

Discussion

This is example discussion text being typed into the discussion box. It should be small enough to fit in the box, but large enough to read. There should be sufficient space between the text and the border.

Number of Problems Reported

Number of Problems Resolved

Cumulative Problems Outstanding

Release Test Comparison (Special)

This daily report shows the problems identified during pre-release of multiple versions of the same application. The report shows a variance analysis of the number of problems reported each day and the number of problems resolved each day. Problems are broken down by priority. Cumulative problems outstanding at the end of the reporting period are shown in the third chart. In addition a break down of the outstanding problems by priority is provided. The report is distributed to the Director of Quality Assurance and to the CIO.

This report will be prepared following each application release, which compares the number of problems identified during pre-release testing and the level of testing effort expended. This will help to measure the quality of new versions of an application.

Metrics

- ◆ Variance Analysis of Problems Reported Prior Release versus Current Release
- ◆ Number of Problems Reported
    - ❐ Priority 1 (Variance Count)
    - ❐ Priority 2 (Variance Count)
    - ❐ Priority 3 (Variance Count)
- ◆ Number of Problems Resolved
    - ❐ Priority 1 (Variance Count)
    - ❐ Priority 2 (Variance Count)
    - ❐ Priority 3 (Variance Count)
- ◆ Number of Problems Outstanding
    - ❐ Priority 1 (Variance Count)
    - ❐ Priority 2 (Variance Count)
    - ❐ Priority 3 (Variance Count)

Release Test Comparison (Special)

Discussion

This is example discussion text being typed into the discussion box. It should be small enough to fit in the box, but large enough to read. There should be sufficient space between the text and the border.

Number of Problems Reported (Variance)

Priority_1 Priority_2 Priority_3

Number of Problems Resolved (Variance)

Priority_1 Priority_2 Priority_3

Cumulative Problems Outstanding (Variance)

Priority_1 Priority_2 Priority_3

221

Customer Satisfaction

This report provides a one page summary of the significant projects within IT. The project report can be used for application development, for hardware implementation, or office automation projects. The report is intended for the CIO, the Project Managers in charge of each significant project, the Executive Committee, and for inclusion in the SLA reporting package for each affected business unit.

Metrics
♦ Number of Customer Complaints Logged
♦ Number of Program Discrepancies Logged
♦ Number of FTE Hours of System Outage
♦ Number of Processing Items Late vs. On-Time

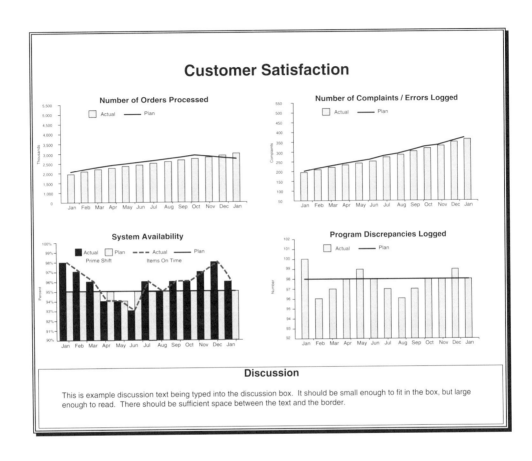

Quality Improvement Program

This report shows the improvement to operations as a direct result of continuous quality improvement projects. The report shows the problem statistics for a given aspect of operations where improvement is needed. Both initial and current statistics are shown. In addition, it shows the planned quality improvement profile. The report is intended for the director of Quality Assurance, the CIO, and the Project Manager in charge of each area.

Metrics
♦ Initial Status of Errors by Type (Count)
♦ Current Status of Errors by Type (Count)
♦ Problems Outstanding Plan (Count)
♦ Problems Outstanding Actual (Count)

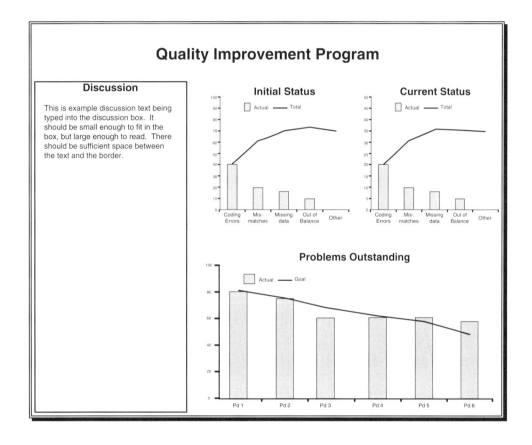

Work Load Summary

This report shows work load levels within the help desk function. It reports on the number of calls handled by the help desk operators, and shows the number of calls per operator. This information can be used to establish appropriate staffing levels for the help desk function. The report also shows the number of incidents that have been reported through the help desk and the number of incidents taken on average by each operator. This report is distributed to the manager in charge of the help desk function and to the CIO.

Metrics
◆ Call Statistics - Incoming Calls (Count)
◆ Call Statistics - Outgoing Calls (Count)
◆ Problem Statistics Incidents (Count)
◆ Problem Statistics Average/Operator (Count)

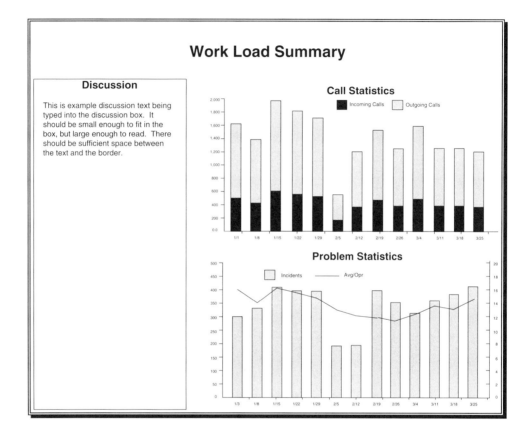

Quick Incidents

This report shows the profile of incidents and how many of those were solved immediately. These later items are known as quick incidents. A vast number of incidents reported through the help desk can be resolved immediately depending on the skill level of the help desk staff. This report is produced weekly and is intended for the Manager of the Help Desk function as well as for the CIO. It shows a three month trend line of the average number of quick incidents per reported incidents.

The discussion frame can be used to explain changes in the trend, such as the increase of call volume, the timing of a new release of software, or the infusion of higher skilled staff for the help desk function. It may be desirable to modify this report to show the quick incidents by type of call, e.g., procedural, hardware operations, software operations, and others.

A quick incident is one in which the help desk receives a call and is able to answer the question within 5 minutes with the caller still on the line

Metrics
◆ Quick Incidents - Incidents (Count)
◆ Quick Incidents - Quick (Count)
◆ Quick Incidents - Moving Average (Percent)

Quick Incidents

Discussion

This is example discussion text being typed into the discussion box. It should be small enough to fit in the box, but large enough to read. There should be sufficient space between the text and the border.

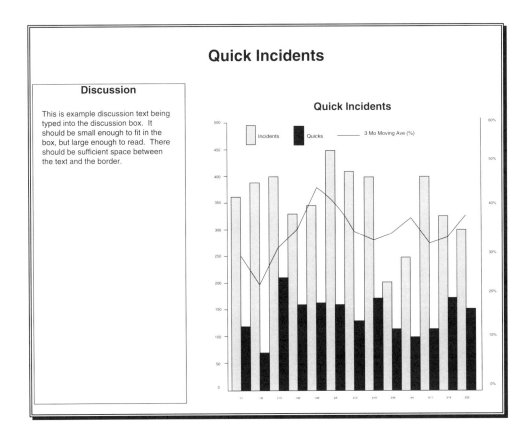

Quick Incidents

Problem Notification Analysis

This report shows the break down of reported problems by source and by market. Both current period and year-to-date actual problem counts are shown in the charts. The first chart shows the source of the problem reported by IT and by the various markets or business units. The second chart breaks down the market reported problems by individual market or business unit. The report is for the Manager of the Help Desk function and for the CIO. The markets or business units experiencing the most problems are easily identifiable from the report's graphics.

Metrics
◆ Problem Notification by Source - Period (Count)
◆ Problem Notification by Source - YTD (Count)
◆ Problem Notification by Customer - Period (Count)
◆ Problem Notification by Customer - YTD (Count)

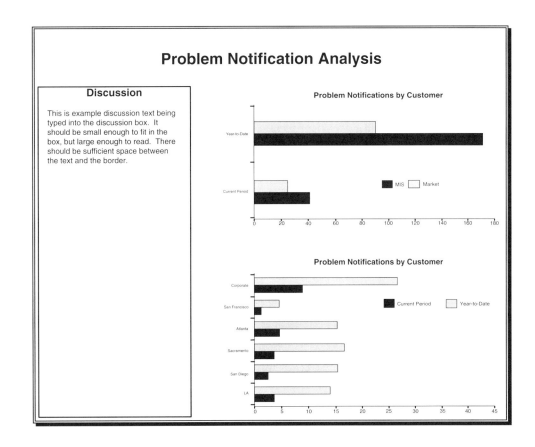

Problem Notification by Priority

This report shows the break down of reported problems by priority. The report has three components. The first component shows the number of reported problems for each reporting period. The second component shows the number of problems closed during each reporting period. The third component is the number of the remaining open problems that are being worked on. A fourth component could be considered on an optional basis. It would provide a break down of the open items by the number of days they have been outstanding. The report is produced monthly but it reflects data on a weekly basis. The report is intended for the Manager of the Help Desk function through which the problems are recorded and resolution is managed. It is also for the CIO. A special version of this report by each market should be produced in support of service level agreements.

There are special procedures for preparing this report relating to the aging analysis.

Problems for purpose of this book are defined:
Priority 1 -- Must fix now, system will not run
Priority 2 -- Need to fix soon, user has a work around
Priority 3 -- Enhancement to the system

Metrics

- ◆ Number Reported
    - ❒ Priority 1 (Count)
    - ❒ Priority 2 (Count)
    - ❒ Priority 3 (Count)
- ◆ Number Closed
    - ❒ Priority 1 (Count)
    - ❒ Priority 2 (Count)
    - ❒ Priority 3 (Count)
- ◆ Number Remaining Open
    - ❒ Priority 1 (Count)
    - ❒ Priority 2 (Count)
    - ❒ Priority 3 (Count)

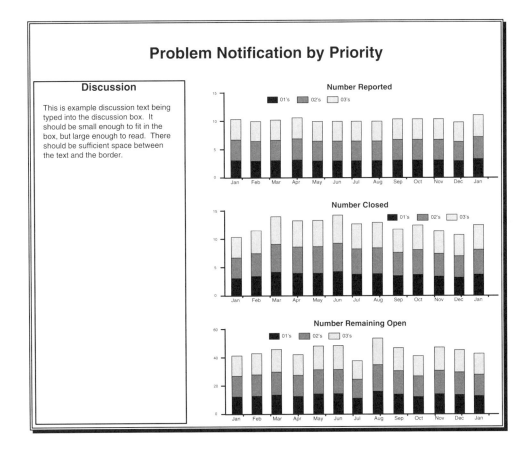

Problem Notification by Priority

Discussion

This is example discussion text being typed into the discussion box. It should be small enough to fit in the box, but large enough to read. There should be sufficient space between the text and the border.

Number Reported

Number Closed

Number Remaining Open

Problem Notification by Category

This report is similar to the Problem Notification by Priority report. It shows the reported problems in the following categories: Hardware, Communications, Software, and Office Automation. The charts on the report show the number of reported problems, the number of closed problems, the number of problems remaining open at the end of the period and the aging of open problems. The report is distributed to the CIO, Manager of the Help Desk function and specific IT Managers or Directors responsible for each of the categories. This report is produced weekly for internal use and monthly to supplement other reporting.

Metrics

- ◆ Number Reported
  - ❏ Hardware (Count)
  - ❏ Communications / LAN (Count)
  - ❏ Office Automation (Count)
  - ❏ Software (Count)
- ◆ Number Closed
  - ❏ Hardware (Count)
  - ❏ Communications / LAN (Count)
  - ❏ Office Automation (Count)
  - ❏ Software (Count)
- ◆ Number Remaining Open
  - ❏ Hardware (Count)
  - ❏ Communications / LAN (Count)
  - ❏ Office Automation (Count)
  - ❏ Software (Count)

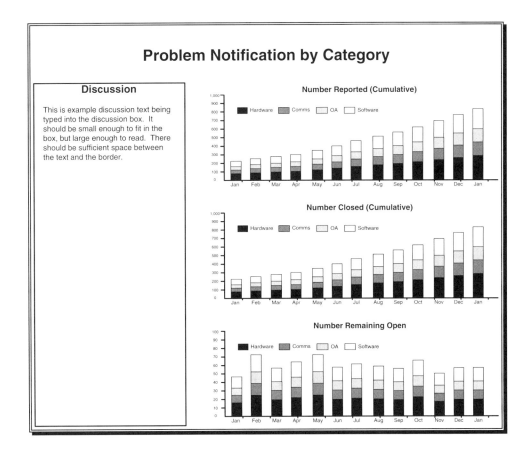

Problem Closure Statistics

This report shows the number of days it takes to close reported problems. The statistics are provided for priority one, two, and three problem notifications. For the priority one problem notification, the service level performance criteria are reflected in the graph. For all problems there is a "days to close" trend line shown on the report. This report is produced monthly. It is distributed to the Manager of the Help Desk function, the CIO and will be incorporated in the SLA feedback reporting to the individual markets.

Problems for purpose of this book are defined:
Priority 1 -- Must fix now, system will not run
Priority 2 -- Need to fix soon, user has a work around
Priority 3 -- Enhancement to the system

Metrics
◆ Priority 1 - Days to Close 80% (Average)
◆ Priority 1 - Days to Close All (Average)
◆ Priority 1 - Days to Close Goal (Average)
◆ Priority 2 & 3 - Days to Close 80% (Average)
◆ Priority 2 &3 - Days to Close All (Average)
◆ Priority 2 & 3 - Days to Close Goal (Average)
◆ Days to Close Trend
❏ Priority 1 (3 Month Moving Average)
❏ Priority 2 (3 Month Moving Average)
❏ Priority 3 (3 Month Moving Average)

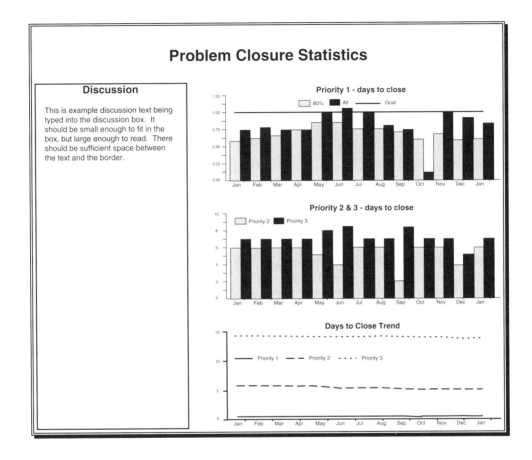

Problem Closure Statistics

Discussion

This is example discussion text being typed into the discussion box. It should be small enough to fit in the box, but large enough to read. There should be sufficient space between the text and the border.

Installation Repair Management

This report supports the Services Level Agreements. There are four measures reported on the report; terminal installation performance, terminal repair performance, printer installation performance and printer repair performance. In each of the four measures the performance goal and the actual performance are shown. This report is produced monthly for distribution to the CIO and the director of computer operations. It is also included in the SLA reporting packages to the individual markets.

Metrics

- Workstation/Terminal[45] Installations All (Average Days)
- Workstation/Terminal Installations 95% (Average Days)
- Workstation/Terminal Installations Low (Quickest Days)
- Workstation/Terminal Installations High (Longest Days)
- Workstation/Terminal Repair All (Average Days)
- Workstation/Terminal Repair 95% (Average Days)
- Workstation/Terminal Repair Low (Quickest Days)
- Workstation/Terminal Repair High (Longest Days)
- Printer Installations All (Average Days)
- Printer Installations 95% (Average Days)
- Printer Installations Low (Quickest Days)
- Printer Installations High (Longest Days)
- Printer Repair All (Average Days)
- Printer Repair 95% (Average Days)
- Printer Repair Low (Quickest Days)
- Printer Repair High (Longest Days)

---

45 Terminal can be a workstation or a PC or any other device that the user uses to communicate with the system.

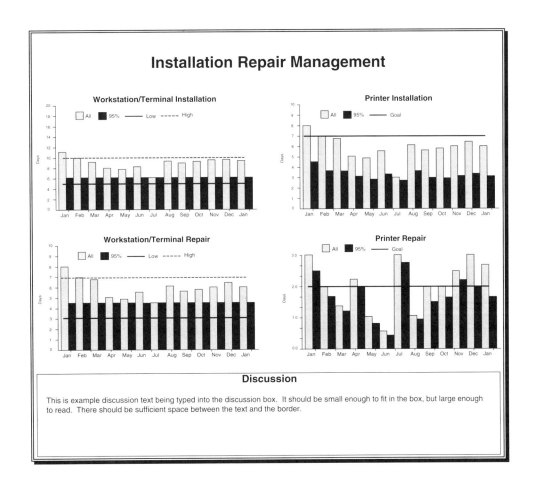

Computer Capacity

This report shows computer resource usage relative to plan. There are two measures reported on this report: CPU usage and DASD or disk usage. For CPU usage, the installed capacity and the acceptable usage limit is shown. Actual usage for the reporting period is shown as an average amount and an average "peak" usage amount. For disc usage, the installed capacity is shown as is the actual average disk usage for the reporting period. Percent utilized is shown in the data tables for both measures. The report is distributed to the CIO and to the director of the computer operations.

Metrics
♦ CPU[46] Usage - MIPS[47] - Peak (Number)
♦ CPU Usage - MIPS - Average (Number)
♦ CPU Usage - MIPS - Maximum (Number)
♦ CPU Usage - MIPS - Acceptable (Number)
♦ DASD[48] Usage - Gigabytes - Maximum (Capacity)
♦ DASD Usage - Gigabytes - Actual (Usage)

46   CPU -- Central Processing Unit is another term for computer
47   MIPS -- Millions of Instructions Per Second
48   DASD -- Direct Access Storage Device is another term for hard disk storage space and a Gigabyte is 1,000 Megabytes of storage space

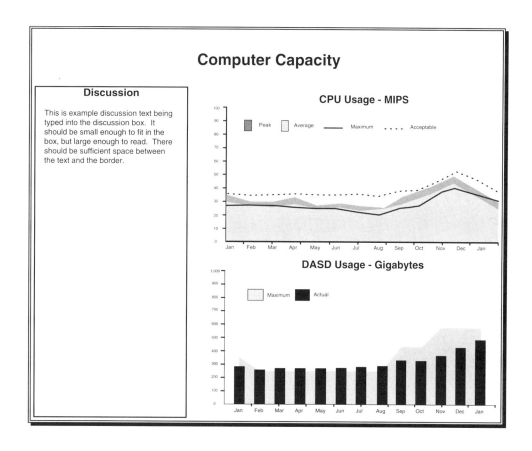

Combined Computer Work Load

This report shows the profile of processing volume that is handled by the IT computer operations function. The number of on-line transactions and the number of batch production jobs are reported. For both of these measures the planned processing volume is shown along side of the actual processing volume. This report is produced monthly and distributed to the CIO and to the director of computer operations.

Volume trends can be added if desired.

Metrics
◆ CPU On-line Transactions - Plan (Count)
◆ CPU On-line Transactions - Actual (Count)
◆ Batch Production Jobs - Plan (Count)
◆ Batch Production Jobs - Actual (Count)

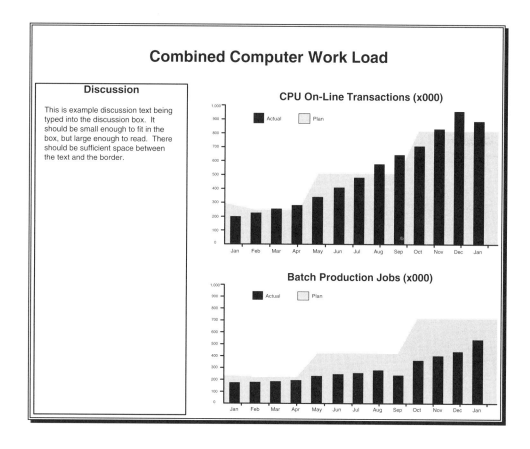

Combined Computer Work Load

Discussion

This is example discussion text being typed into the discussion box. It should be small enough to fit in the box, but large enough to read. There should be sufficient space between the text and the border.

CPU On-Line Transactions (x000)

Actual   Plan

Jan Feb Mar Apr May Jun Jul Aug Sep Oct Nov Dec Jan

Batch Production Jobs (x000)

Actual   Plan

Jan Feb Mar Apr May Jun Jul Aug Sep Oct Nov Dec Jan

On-Line Performance Summary

This report shows computer availability in support of on-line operations and to show on-line response time from an end user's perspective. Both of these measures are needed to support the service level agreements. For both measures the performance goal and the actual performance are reflected in the graphs. For the on-line response time, both an average response time and a response time for ninety percent of all on-line transactions is provided. This report is produced monthly and distributed to the CIO and the director of computer operations. It is also included in the SLA reporting package for the individual markets.

If the markets are processed on different computers or computer clusters, then separate reports should be produced for each SLA market reporting package.

Metrics
♦ On-Line Availability - Plan (Percent)
♦ On-Line Availability - Actual (Percent)
♦ On-Line Response Time - Plan (Seconds)
♦ On-Line Response Time -Average (Seconds)
♦ On-Line Response Time - 90% (Seconds)

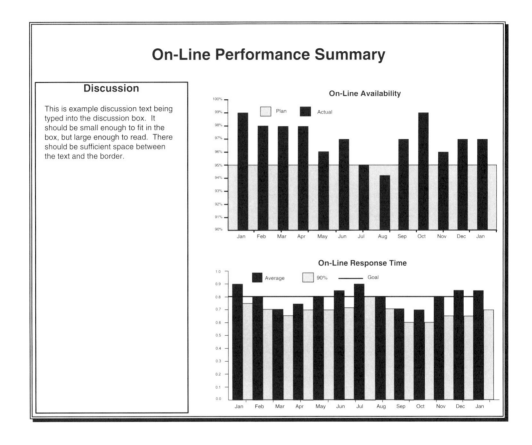

E-Mail and EDI Traffic

This report provides a one page summary of the E-Mail traffic and EDI transactions within IT. The report is intended for the CIO, the Project Managers in charge of each significant project, the Executive Committee, and for inclusion in the SLA reporting package for each affected business unit.

Metrics

- ♦ Internal E-Mail Messages - Sent/Received
- ♦ External E-Mail Messages - Sent/Received
- ♦ EDI Transactions (Dollars/Count)

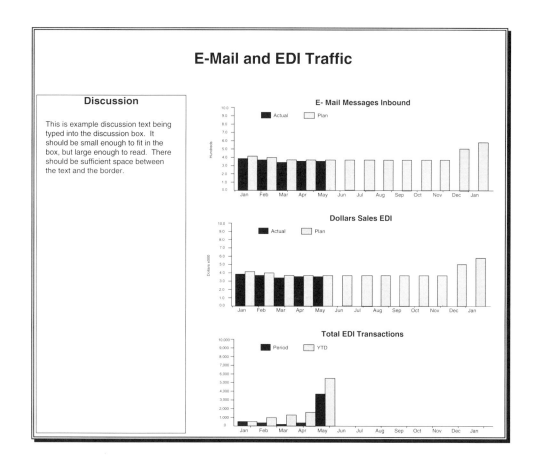

Computer Outages

This report shows the number of outages and the total amount of the time the computer was unavailable to support on-line, prime time operations. The report also shows the average amount of time it takes for IT to resolve these outages. This report is produced in total by month for the IT operations department. In addition, separate reports are produced for each market to show performance of the computer and responsiveness of the IT computer operation support staff. The report is distributed to the CIO, the director of computer operations and to the market representatives as part of SLA reporting.

Metrics

- ◆ Number of Outages (Count)
- ◆ Total Outage Time (Minutes)
- ◆ Average Resolution Time - Goal (Minutes)
- ◆ Average Resolution Time - Average (Minutes)

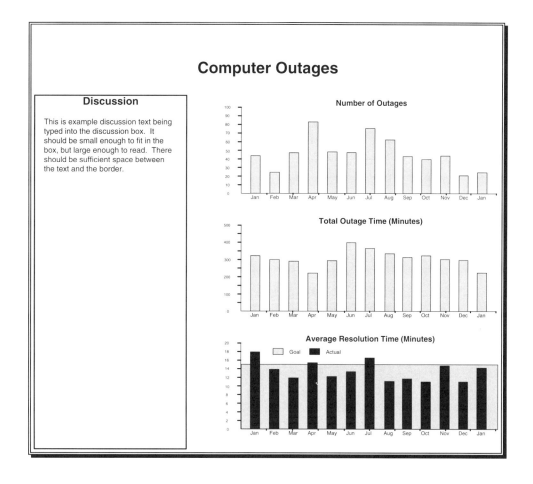

Batch Processing Performance

This report shows the performance of the computer operations department in processing batch jobs. Two measures are reported; the billing batch performance and the batch performance for processing other specific jobs such as vendor tapes. Both of these measures are specified in the Services Level Agreement. The charts reflect both the target performance level and the actual performance achieved. This report is distributed monthly to the CIO, the director of computer operations and the individual markets as part of the SLA reporting.

This report is produced in total for IT operations and by individual market. The details of processing individual job types are reported on an attached detailed status report.

Metrics
◆   Main Batch Processing Performance - Plan (%)
◆   Main Batch Processing Performance - Actual (%)

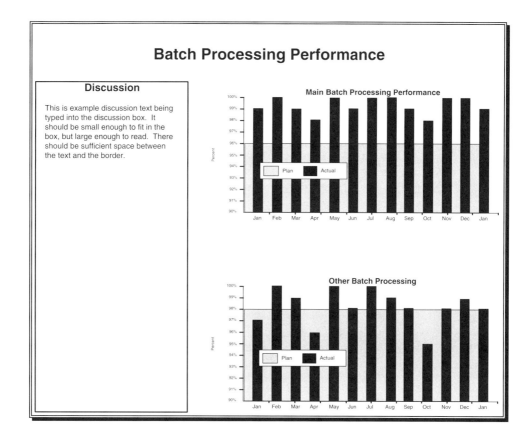

Billing & Report Distribution Performance

This report supports the Service Level Agreements. There are two measures on this report. The first one is billing performance in terms of number of days early or late. The second measure is the number of reports delivered to the market on time. Both charts reflect the service level target and the actual performance level achieved for the period. This monthly report is produced in total for IT Operations as well as by market. The report is distributed to the CIO and the director of computer operations; it will be included in the SLA Reporting Package to the individual markets.

It is suggested that the billing performance calculations be based on dollars-days early or late rather than numbers of days early or late. This approach allows for averaging across the month, and across more than one billing cycle. This would result in a fairer measure of IT performance and relate the IT performance to the dollar impact on the corporation.

Metrics
♦ Billing Performance - Days Early/Late Actual
♦ Billing Performance - Days Early/Late Plan
♦ Reports Delivered on Time Plan (Percent)
♦ Reports Delivered on Time Actual (Percent)

Billing & Report Distribution Performance

Discussion

This is example discussion text being typed into the discussion box. It should be small enough to fit in the box, but large enough to read. There should be sufficient space between the text and the border.

Billing Performance - Days Early / Late

Plan — Actual ☐

Reports Delivered on Time

Plan ☐ Actual ■

253

Charge Back Details

The purpose of this report is to show the break down of the IT charge back for each market or operating unit by the type of resource. A similar report will be prepared for each market or operating unit.

This report is intended to support the IT cost allocation or charge back policies and should be included in the SLA reporting package.

This report must be integrated with a charge back system. In addition to each individual report, there should be one report that summarizes all charge backs for the enterprise.

Metrics

♦ Billings by Department YTD (Percent)

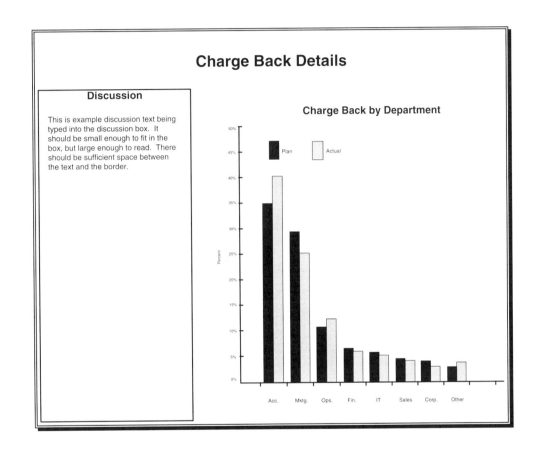

Charge Back Details

Discussion

This is example discussion text being typed into the discussion box. It should be small enough to fit in the box, but large enough to read. There should be sufficient space between the text and the border.

Charge Back by Department

Network Outages

This report shows the number of outages and the total amount of the time the network was unavailable to support on-line, prime time operations. The report also shows the average amount of time it takes for IT to resolve these outages. This report is produced in total by month for the IT operations department. In addition, separate reports are produced for each market to show performance of the network and responsiveness of the IT network operation support staff. The report is distributed to the CIO, the director of computer operations and to the market representatives as part of SLA reporting.

There should be version of this report produced for each network (perhaps LAN) node in the enterprise.

Metrics
♦ Number of Outages (Count)
♦ Total Outage Time (Minutes)
♦ Average Resolution Time - Goal (Minutes)
♦ Average Resolution Time - Average (Minutes)

Network Outages

Discussion

This is example discussion text being typed into the discussion box. It should be small enough to fit in the box, but large enough to read. There should be sufficient space between the text and the border.

Number of Outages

Total Outage Time (Minutes)

Average Resolution Time (Minutes)

Electronic Commerce

This report provides a one page summary of the significant projects within IT. The project report can be used for application development, for hardware implementation, or office automation projects. The report is intended for the CIO, the Project Managers in charge of each significant project, the Executive Committee, and for inclusion in the SLA reporting package for each affected business unit.

Much has been written on project management. The one lesson we have learned is the value of a single page report that summarizes time, cost and staffing.

Metrics

- ♦ Internal E-Mail Messages - Sent/Received
- ♦ External E-Mail Messages - Sent/Received
- ♦ EDI Transactions (Dollars/Count)

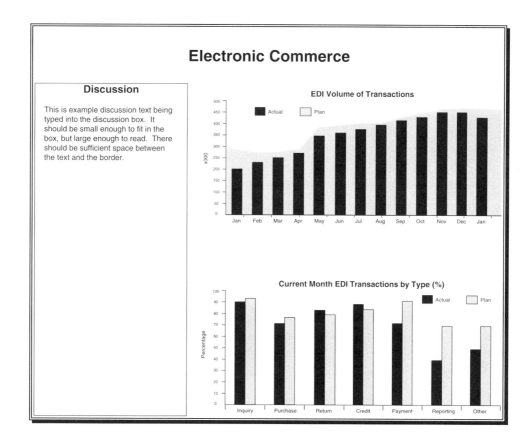

Electronic Commerce

Discussion

This is example discussion text being typed into the discussion box. It should be small enough to fit in the box, but large enough to read. There should be sufficient space between the text and the border.

EDI Volume of Transactions

Actual ▪ Plan ☐

Current Month EDI Transactions by Type (%)

Actual ▪ Plan ☐

Switch Performance Report

Each switch has it own unique throughput issues. A report on the performance of it should be produced. The purpose of this metric is to identify when a switch has reached its capacity and needs to be upgraded.

In addition a Switch Outage report could be produced if that is an issue. We have found if this is the case the switch will be moved out before the metric is in place. By that time the metric is not worth the effort of production. The only purpose would be to provide documentation of improved switch performance.

Metrics
◆ Number of Trunks Busy Plan
◆ Number of Trunks Busy Actual
◆ Agents on Call Plan
◆ Agents on Call Actual

Switch Performance Report

Discussion

This is example discussion text being typed into the discussion box. It should be small enough to fit in the box, but large enough to read. There should be sufficient space between the text and the border.

Number of Trunks Busy

Agents on Call

Voice Mail Performance

The purpose of this report is to show the usage of the voice mail system. The number of users and percentage of disk full can be used to forecast the necessary points for system upgrades.

If multiple voice mail systems are in place in an enterprise, then this report could be used to identify candidate systems and equipment re-distribution within the enterprise.

Metrics
◆ Number of Users Plan (Count)
◆ Number of Users Actual (Count)
◆ Percentage of Disk Full (Percent)

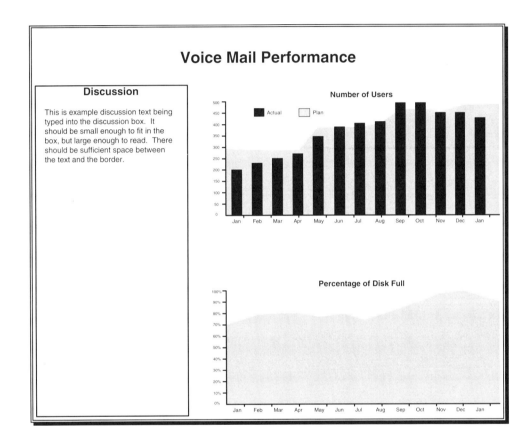

Voice Mail Performance

Discussion

This is example discussion text being typed into the discussion box. It should be small enough to fit in the box, but large enough to read. There should be sufficient space between the text and the border.

Number of Users

Percentage of Disk Full

Workstation Analysis

The purpose of this report is to show the extent to which IT workstations have been introduced into the organization. Information is provided on the total use of personal computers and standard computer terminals. This information is intended for the CIO and his presentation to the Corporate Executive Committee.

The information in this report is used in the calculation of the comparisons to annual industry survey statistics. Where possible, this report should be produced as a comparative report to an enterprise's primary and secondary competitors.

In many enterprises this report may be produced once a year instead of quarterly. In most organizations, monthly reporting is overkill and quarterly reporting is preferred.

Metrics
◆ Number of Workstations - Plan (Count)
◆ Number of Workstations - Actual (Count)
◆ Workstation Penetration by Department Plan (%)
◆ Workstation Penetration by Department Actual (%)

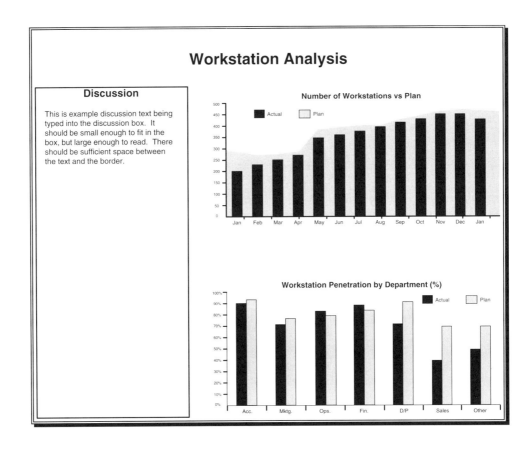

Workstation Analysis

Discussion

This is example discussion text being typed into the discussion box. It should be small enough to fit in the box, but large enough to read. There should be sufficient space between the text and the border.

LAN Analysis

The purpose of this report is to show the extent to which IT LANs have been introduced into the organization. Information is provided on the average and maximum number of users. This information is intended for the CIO and his presentation to the Corporate Executive Committee.

The information in this report is used in the calculation of the comparisons to annual industry survey statistics. Where possible, this report should be produced as a comparative report to an enterprise's primary and secondary competitors.

In many enterprises this report may be produced once a year instead of quarterly. In most organizations, monthly reporting is overkill and quarterly reporting is preferred.

Metrics
◆ Number of Users - Plan (Count)
◆ Number of Users - Actual (Count)
◆ Maximum Number of Users- Plan (Count)
◆ Maximum Number of Users Actual (Count)

LAN Analysis

Discussion

This is example discussion text being typed into the discussion box. It should be small enough to fit in the box, but large enough to read. There should be sufficient space between the text and the border.

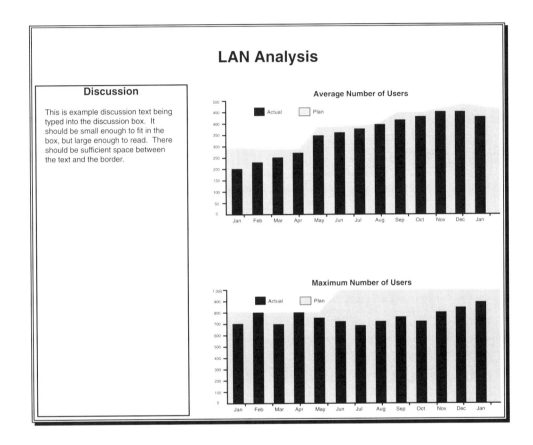

Usage Analysis

The purpose of this report is to show the extent to which IT PCs have been introduced into the organization. Information is provided on the use of personal computers by department and in total. This information is intended for the CIO and his presentation to the Corporate Executive Committee.

One version of this report may be by type of PC (486, Pentium pro, Alpha, Mips, Mac, UNIX, etc.); the software (123, Excel, etc.) on a PC; or the type of software (spread sheets, databases, word processors, etc.) on each PC.

The information in this report is used in the calculation of the comparisons to annual industry survey statistics. Where possible, this report should be produced as a comparative report to an enterprise's primary and secondary competitors.

In many enterprises this report may be produced once a quarterly. In most organizations, monthly reporting is overkill.

Metrics
♦ Number - Plan (Count)
♦ Number - Actual (Count)
♦ Penetration by Department Plan (%)
♦ Penetration by Department Actual (%)

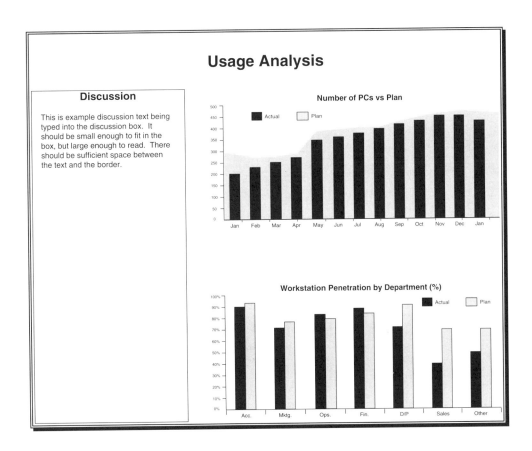

Distribution

Metrics which are specific to the distribution industry and specific enterprises in that industry need to be related to IT in such a way that the metric shows the value versus cost of IT in enterprise terms. Below are some metrics that we have found useful. Some of these metrics can be used in other industries. Only one sample report is depicted on the following page.

Metrics

- ♦ Quantity Shipped (#Trucks) (Plan/Actual)
- ♦ Cost Per Unit Shipped (or x000) IT Expense - Plan
- ♦ Cost Per Unit Shipped (or x000) IT Expense - Actual
- ♦ Number Bills of Lading (Plan/Actual)
- ♦ Cost Per Bill of Lading (Plan/Actual)
- ♦ Service Level Percent (Plan)
- ♦ Service Level Actual (Actual)
- ♦ Days (or $) Inventory - Received (Plan/Actual)
- ♦ Days (or $) Inventory - Shipped (Plan/Actual)
- ♦ Days (or $) Inventory - On Hand (Plan/Actual)
- ♦ Order/Return Throughput
    - ❑ Number of Orders Processed
    - ❑ Number of Returns
    - ❑ Number of Distribution Orders
- ♦ Order/Return Handling
    - ❑ Orders On Time
    - ❑ Returns Processed On Time
    - ❑ Distribution Orders On Time
- ♦ Stock/Warehouse/Shipping Performance
    - ❑ Picking Accuracy
    - ❑ Bin Level Inventory Accuracy
    - ❑ Parcel Accuracy
    - ❑ Percentage Audits Passed
- ♦ Timeliness Of EDI Transmissions
    - ❑ On Time EDI Transmissions (TO)
    - ❑ On Time EDI Transmissions (FROM)
    - ❑ On Time Reports to Customers
    - ❑ On Time Scheduled Data Transmission
- ♦ Distribution Activity by Production Source (Actual Vs. Forecast)
    - ❑ New Product Orders
    - ❑ Promotions
    - ❑ Restocking Orders
    - ❑ Other Orders

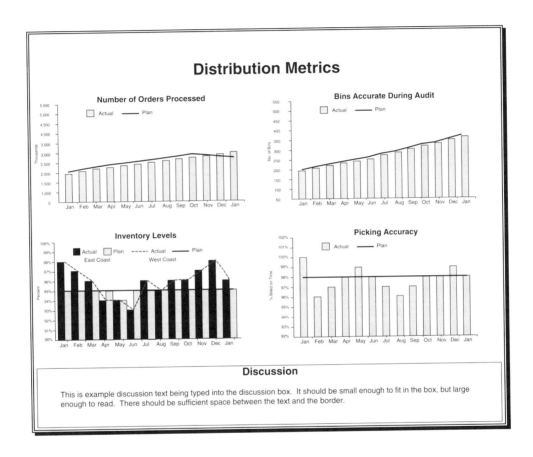

Education

Metrics which are specific to the education industry and specific enterprises in that industry need to be related to IT in such a way that the metric shows the value versus cost of IT in enterprise terms. These same metrics could be used for an internal training department. Below are some metrics that we have found useful. Some of these metrics can be used in other industries. Only one sample report is depicted on the following page.

Metrics
♦ Student Electronic Hours (Plan/Actual)
♦ Cost Per Student (Plan/Actual)
♦ Number Electronic Transactions (Plan/Actual)
♦ Number Of Electronic Customer Interactions
♦ Training Quality Goals
❏ Satisfaction Survey Results
❏ Average Number of Weeks for Training
❏ Percentage Completing Training
❏ Absenteeism Index
❏ Unused Sick Days
❏ Unused Vacation Days

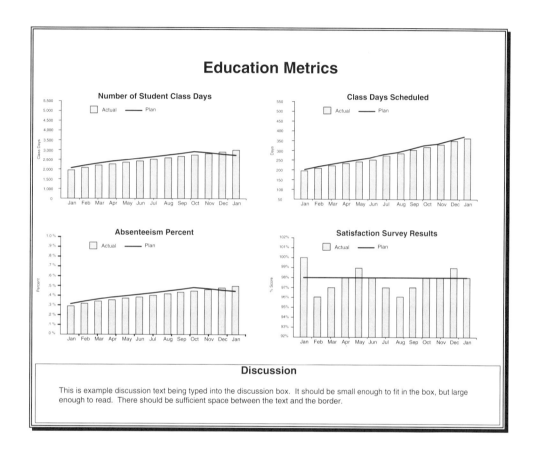

Education Metrics

Number of Student Class Days

Actual — Plan

Class Days Scheduled

Actual — Plan

Absenteeism Percent

Actual — Plan

Satisfaction Survey Results

Actual — Plan

Discussion

This is example discussion text being typed into the discussion box. It should be small enough to fit in the box, but large enough to read. There should be sufficient space between the text and the border.

Entertainment

Metrics which are specific to the entertainment industry and specific enterprises in that industry need to be related to IT in such a way that the metric shows the value versus cost of IT in enterprise terms. Below are some metrics that we have found useful. Some of these metrics can be used in other industries. Only one sample report is depicted on the following page.

Metrics

- ◆ Quantity Shipped (Plan/Actual)
- ◆ Cost Per Unit Shipped (or x000) IT Expense - Plan
- ◆ Cost Per Unit Shipped (or x000) IT Expense - Actual
- ◆ Number Title (Plan/Actual)
- ◆ Cost Per Title (Plan/Actual)
- ◆ Service Level Percent (Plan)
- ◆ Service Level Actual (Actual)
- ◆ Days (or $) Inventory - Received (Plan/Actual)
- ◆ Days (or $) Inventory - Shipped (Plan/Actual)
- ◆ Days (or $) Inventory - On Hand (Plan/Actual)
- ◆ Title Performance
  - ❐ Year To Date Unit Shipments
  - ❐ Inception To Date Unit Shipments
  - ❐ Net Unit Sales – Titles (Inventory) Assets (Net of Returns)

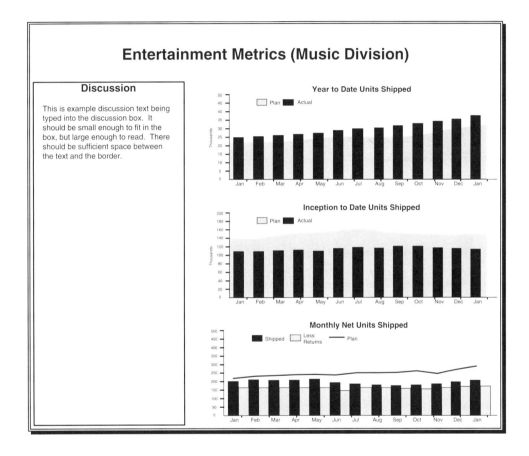

Entertainment Metrics (Music Division)

Discussion

This is example discussion text being typed into the discussion box. It should be small enough to fit in the box, but large enough to read. There should be sufficient space between the text and the border.

Year to Date Units Shipped

Inception to Date Units Shipped

Monthly Net Units Shipped

Financial Service

Metrics which are specific to the financial service industry and specific enterprises in that industry need to be related to IT in such a way that the metric shows the value versus cost of IT in enterprise terms. Below are some metrics that we have found useful. Some of these metrics can be used in other industries. Only one sample report is depicted on the following page.

Metrics

- ♦ Number Transactions (Plan/Actual)
- ♦ Cost Per Transaction(or x000) IT Expense - Plan
- ♦ Cost Per Transaction (or x000) IT Expense - Actual
- ♦ Dollar Volume Electronic Transactions (Plan/Actual)
- ♦ Average Size of Electronic Transaction (Plan/Actual)
- ♦ Service Level Percent (Plan)
- ♦ Service Level Actual (Actual)
- ♦ Number E-Mail Messages Inbound
- ♦ Number E-Mail Messages Outbound
- ♦ Customer Satisfaction
  - ❐ Satisfaction Index
  - ❐ Percentage of Repeat Customers This Period
  - ❐ Percentage of Customer With No Activity in the Last Two Periods
  - ❐ Repeat Customer - Order Size Larger Current Period Versus Prior Period

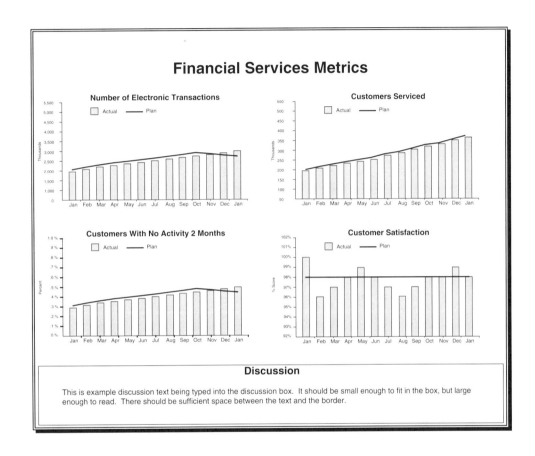

Government

Metrics which are specific to the government sector (federal, state and local) and specific enterprises in that industry need to be related to IT in such a way that the metric shows the value versus cost of IT in enterprise terms. Below are some metrics that we have found useful. Some of these metrics can be used in other industries. Only one sample report is depicted on the following page.

Metrics
◆ Customer[49] Count (Plan/Actual)
◆ Cost Per Customer (Plan/Actual)
◆ Dollar Volume (Plan/Actual)
◆ Number Electronic Transactions (Plan/Actual)
◆ Dollar Volume Electronic Transactions (Plan/Actual
◆ Number of Electronic Customer Interactions
◆ Number of Transactions Processed[50]
◆ WEB Page Inquires
◆ E-Mail Volume

---

[49] Customer count is "encounter" between the government entity and the user of the governmental service.
[50] Not included on the sample chart

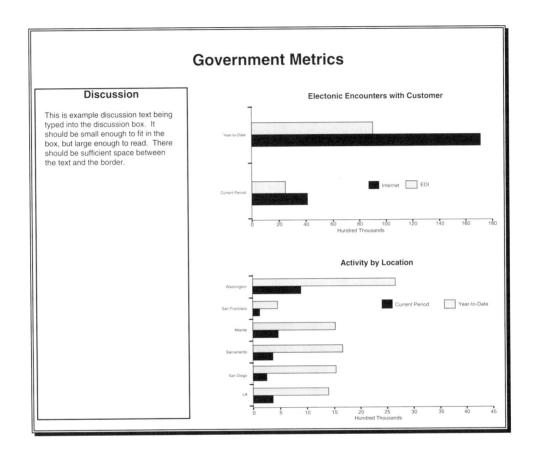

Government Metrics

Discussion

This is example discussion text being typed into the discussion box. It should be small enough to fit in the box, but large enough to read. There should be sufficient space between the text and the border.

Electonic Encounters with Customer

Activity by Location

Hospitality

Metrics which are specific to the hospitality industry and specific enterprises in that industry need to be related to IT in such a way that the metric shows the value versus cost of IT in enterprise terms. Below are some metrics that we have found useful. Some of these metrics can be used in other industries. Only one sample report is depicted on the following page.

Metrics

- ♦ Customer Count (Plan/Actual)
- ♦ Dollar Volume (Plan/Actual)
- ♦ Cost Per Customer (Plan/Actual)
- ♦ Number Electronic Transactions (Plan/Actual)
- ♦ Dollar Volume Electronic Transactions (Plan/Actual
- ♦ Number of Electronic Customer Interactions
- ♦ Customer Satisfaction Index
  - ❏ Customer Counts
  - ❏ Repeat Customers
  - ❏ Credits
  - ❏ Sales
  - ❏ Customer Service Complaints

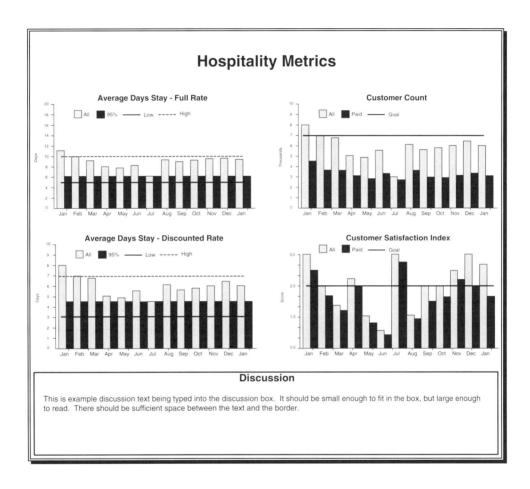

Insurance

Metrics which are specific to the insurance industry and specific enterprises in that industry need to be related to IT in such a way that the metric shows the value versus cost of IT in enterprise terms. Below are some metrics that we have found useful. Some of these metrics can be used in other industries. Only one sample report is depicted on the following page.

Metrics

- ◆ Number Transactions (Plan/Actual)
- ◆ Cost Per Transaction(or x000) IT Expense - Plan
- ◆ Cost Per Transaction (or x000) IT Expense - Actual
- ◆ Dollar Volume Electronic Transactions (Plan/Actual)
- ◆ Average Size of Electronic Transaction (Plan/Actual)
- ◆ Service Level Percent (Plan)
- ◆ Service Level Actual (Actual)
- ◆ Number E-Mail Messages Inbound
- ◆ Number E-Mail Messages Outbound
- ◆ Business Supported
  - ❐ Number of Lines of Insurance Supported
  - ❐ Cost Per Policy Per Line of Business
  - ❐ Number of Days Required to Process Various Claims (Simple, Average, Complex)
  - ❐ Number of Employees Per Policy Per Line of Business

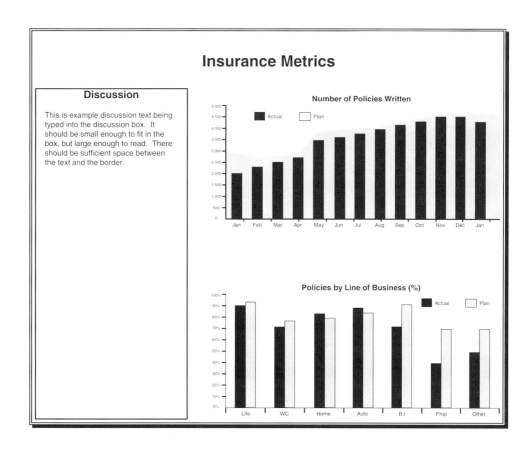

Insurance Metrics

Discussion

This is example discussion text being typed into the discussion box. It should be small enough to fit in the box, but large enough to read. There should be sufficient space between the text and the border.

Number of Policies Written

Policies by Line of Business (%)

Manufacturing

Metrics which are specific to the manufacturing industry and specific enterprises in that industry need to be related to IT in such a way that the metric shows the value versus cost of IT in enterprise terms. Below are some metrics that we have found useful. Some of these metrics can be used in other industries. Only one sample report is depicted on the following page.

Metrics   ·

- ◆ Quantity Manufactured (Plan/Actual)
- ◆ Number Production Orders (Plan/Actual)
- ◆ Number Orders Late/Under (Plan/Actual)
- ◆ Cost Per Unit (or x000) IT Expense - Plan
- ◆ Cost Per Unit (or x000) IT Expense - Actual
- ◆ Service Level Percent (Plan)
- ◆ Service Level Actual (Actual)
- ◆ Days (or $) Inventory - Raw Material (Plan/Actual)
- ◆ Days (or $) Inventory - In Process (Plan/Actual)
- ◆ Days (or $) Inventory - Finished Goods (Plan/Actual)
- ◆ Manufacturing Goals
    - ❐ Manufacturing Defect Returns
    - ❐ Scrap
    - ❐ Machine Down Time
    - ❐ Set-Up Variances
    - ❐ Production Quality - % Products Returned For Rework
    - ❐ Production Quality - %Products Rejected by Customers

Manufacturing Metrics

Discussion

This is example discussion text being typed into the discussion box. It should be small enough to fit in the box, but large enough to read. There should be sufficient space between the text and the border.

Number Work Orders Completed

Number Finished Goods Needing Rework

Number Finished Goods Rejected by Customers

Medical

Metrics which are specific to the medical/health care industry and specific enterprises in that industry need to be related to IT in such a way that the metric shows the value versus cost of IT in enterprise terms. Below are some metrics that we have found useful. Some of these metrics can be used in other industries. Only one sample report is depicted on the following page.

Metrics
♦ Patient Days Count (Plan/Actual)
♦ Dollar Volume by Department (Plan/Actual)
♦ Cost Per Patient (Plan/Actual)
♦ Number Electronic Transactions (Plan/Actual)
♦ Dollar Volume Electronic Transactions (Plan/Actual
♦ Number of Electronic Customer Interactions
♦ Quantity of Service Provided
❐ Number of Patient Days
❐ Number of Lab Tests by Department
❐ Number of Complaints
❐ Number of Encounters

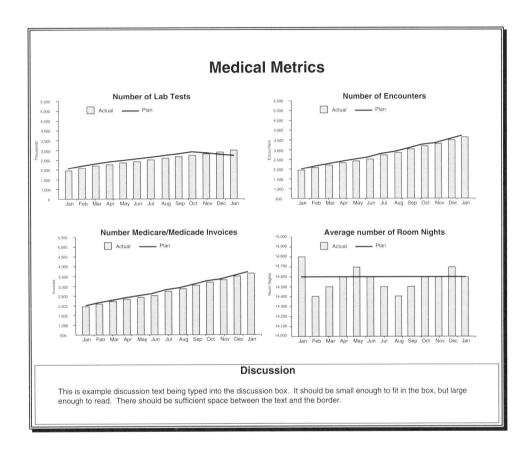

Real Estate

Metrics which are specific to the real estate industry and specific enterprises in that industry need to be related to IT in such a way that the metric shows the value versus cost of IT in enterprise terms. Below are some metrics that we have found useful. Some of these metrics can be used in other industries. Only one sample report is depicted on the following page.

Metrics
◆ Number Leases/Sales (Plan/Actual)
◆ Cost Per Lease/Sale (or x000) IT Expense - Plan
◆ Cost Per Lease/Sale (or x000) IT Expense - Actual
◆ Dollar Volume Electronic Transactions (Plan/Actual)
◆ Average Size of Electronic Transaction (Plan/Actual)
◆ Service Level Percent (Plan)
◆ Service Level Actual (Actual)
◆ Number E-Mail Messages Inbound
◆ Number E-Mail Messages Outbound
◆ Volume of Business
❐ Number of New Agreements Signed
❐ Number and Dollar Value of Sales
❐ Square Footage Available to Lease

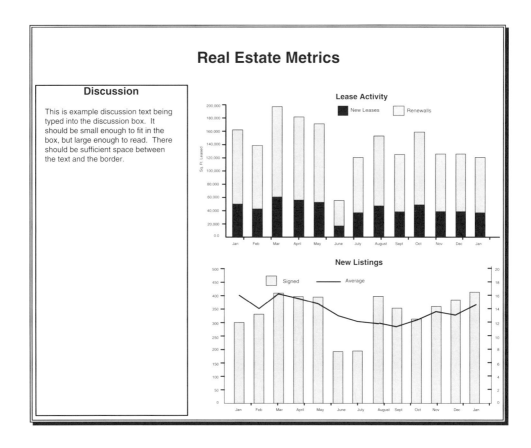

Retail

Metrics which are specific to the retail industry and specific enterprises in that industry need to be related to IT in such a way that the metric shows the value versus cost of IT in enterprise terms. Below are some metrics that we have found useful. Some of these metrics can be used in other industries. Only one sample report is depicted on the following page.

Metrics
◆ Customer Count (Plan/Actual)
◆ Dollar Volume by Product Line (Plan/Actual)
◆ Cost Per Customer (Plan/Actual)
◆ Number Electronic Transactions (Plan/Actual)
◆ Dollar Volume Electronic Transactions (Plan/Actual
◆ Number of Electronic Customer Interactions
◆ Customer Satisfaction
❐ Combined Customer Satisfaction Index
❐ Missed Due Dates For Order Processing
❐ Returns Disposition (Turn-Around Time)
❐ Credit Disposition (Turn-Around Time)
◆ Warehouse Goals
❐ Inventory Accuracy - % Locations at 99.5%
❐ Average Cycle Time - Time to Re-Stock
❐ On Time Shipped Orders
❐ Number of Returns Authorized Above Targets

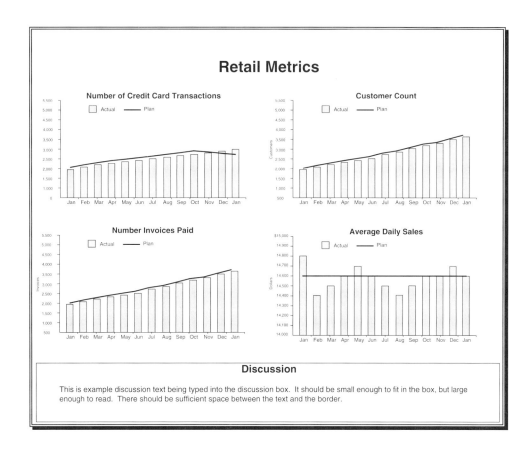

Appendix

Glossary

386DX Another name for Intel's 80386 microprocessor which processes 32 bits of information at a time. Intel's scaled-down version of the 80386, known as the 386SX, can process instructions in memory 32 bits at a time, but only passes information along the I/O bus 16 bits at a time.

486DX Another name for Intel's 80486 microprocessor which processes 32 bits of information at a time. Intel's scaled-down version of the 80486, known as the 486SX, can process instructions in memory 32 bits at a time, but only passes information along the I/O bus 16 bits at a time.

486DX2 Another name for Intel's 80486 microprocessor which processes 32 bits of information at a time but at a clock doubled performance (e.g., 33 MHz becomes 66 MHz).

486DX4 Another name for Intel's 80486 microprocessor which processes 32 bits of information at a time but at a clock tripled performance (e.g., 33 MHz becomes 100 MHz).

Access The operation of seeking, reading, or writing data on a storage unit.

Access Areas Regions partitioned by physical barriers with regulated access points established to ensure separation of duties and enforcement of the principle of least privilege. Individuals should not be allowed access to these controlled areas without specific authorization.

Access Control The process of limiting access to the resources of an information system to only authorized users, programs, processes or other systems (in computer networks).

Access Time The time required for a computer to locate data and move it into the central processing unit.

Accountability The quality or state which enables violations or attempted violations of system security to be traced to individuals who may then be held responsible.

Add-in Cards Circuit boards that allow the user to upgrade or add features to a PC.

Address The code used to designate a specific piece of data within computer storage.

Address Spaces Allocation of virtual memory within the system. The operating system must control each address space so that it passes and receives only those resources specifically authorized and required for its specific function.

ALE Annual Loss Expectancy

American National Standards Institute	ANSI
Annual Loss Expectancy	ALE - An annualized estimate of loss for a single occurrence of an undesirable event as calculated from the probability of occurrence of that event and the loss exposure of that occurrence.
ANSI	Acronym for American National Standards Institute, a governmental organization that proposes, modifies, approves, and publishes IT standards for voluntary use in the United States.
ANSI	American National Standards Institute
APPLE TALK	An inexpensive local area network that allows computers to share files and printers. It is built into every Macintosh, but can also be used with other computers.
Application	A software program or program package that makes calls to the operating system and manipulates data files, thus allowing a user to perform a specific job (such as accounting or word processing).
Application Program	A program that provides directions for the system on the handling of a set of process-unique instructions intended to perform specific operations on application-related data.
Application Server	A PC with applications accessed by the LAN.
Archive	To back up data files. See also Back-Up.
ASCII	(American National) Standard Code for Information Interchange); a generic code representing alphanumeric characters that permits the exchange of text between different operating systems.
Asset Analysis	As part of the risk management process, an inventory of enterprise client server and IT assets (e.g., equipment, software, supplies, documentation) in support of the system, process or facility under study.
Attach	To access a file server; particularly to access additional file servers after having already logged in to one file server. The term also means to connect components, often by cable.
Attribute	See File Attributes.
Audit	To conduct the independent review and examination of system records and activities in order to test for adequacy of system controls, to ensure compliance with established policy and operational procedures, and to recommend any indicated changes in controls, policy or procedures.

Audit Trail	A chronological record of system activities which is sufficient to enable the reconstruction, review and examination of the sequence of events and activities surrounding or leading to each event in the path of a transaction from its inception to output of final results.
Authentication	The process used before granting access to system resources available at the host computer to verify users or jobs requesting access.
Authorization	The process by which an individual establishes a need to know or to have access and, in keeping with the principle of least privilege, is formally authorized to seek access to a controlled area.
Authorization Verification	The process by which an individual, whose identity has been authenticated, is granted the right to access and certain privileges associated with that access.
Autoflow	A feature in page-layout programs that automatically flows text from column to column, or page to page.
Autotrace	A feature in illustration programs that automatically traces bit mapped images to create drawn objects.
Back-up (noun)	A stored copy of a file, directory, or volume preserved as a safeguard in case the original is accidentally corrupted or destroyed.
Back-up (verb)	To copy a file, directory, or volume onto another storage device so that the data may be retrieved if the original source is accidentally corrupted or destroyed. Also known as archiving.
Background Printing	The ability to print a document while running another application.
Baseline	An imaginary line on which the letters in a line of type sit.
BASIC	(Beginner's All-purpose Symbolic Instruction Code) A simplified language for programming a computer, widely used for microcomputer instructions.
Batch File	A file containing commands that can cause several different programs to execute automatically.
Batch Message Processing	BMP - A program which runs in a dependent region of an IMS or DB/2 control region, and has access to OS files as well as IMS or DB/2 data bases and message queues.
BAUD	The unit used to measure the speed of data communications. 10 baud is roughly equivalent to 1 character per second.
BAUD RATE	Also referred to as BPS (bits per second). Refers to the speed at which a modem can transmit data. Divide the baud rate by 10 to get an approximate idea of how many characters per second (CPS) the modem is transmitting. A 1200-baud modem transmits approximately 120 CPS.

BBS
(Bulletin Board System); a computer that has been set up to facilitate the exchange of information among other computers via modem. Often, a service bureau will set up a BBS so that its clients can submit files for output.

Bezier Curve
A curve used in illustration programs that provides control handles for manipulating the shape of the arc; named after cathedral shades in Bezier, France.

BIOS
(Basic Input/Output System) ROM software.

Bit
An on or off state in storage representing a binary digit (0 or 1).

Bit Map
A matrix of dots of the same density that form an image.

Bit Mapped
Graphic images formed by dots; the software producing these images is often referred to as 'paint-type' software.

Bleed
Image that continues off the edge of a page.

Block
A set of data transferred as a unit between components of a computer system. A block may include one or more records.

BMP
Batch Message Processing

Boot (boot up)
To load a computer's operating system into RAM. After the operating system has been booted, applications can be loaded into the computer. See also Cold Boot; Remote Reset; and Warm Boot.

BPS
(Bits Per Second) A unit of measurement that measures the speed of data being transferred over telephone lines. Another term for BPS is BAUD.

Bridge
See LAN Bridge

Buffer
Storage used to compensate for differences in the rates of transfer of data or in the timing of transmission of data from one device to another.

Bug
An inadvertent mistake in the logic of a computer program or in the wiring of a circuit.

Burst Mode
High-speed data transfer that is a feature of Intel's i486 microprocessor.

Bus
A central set of highly specialized electrical sockets within the computer into which virtually all of its circuits and devices are connected.

Byte
A set of eight (8) adjacent bits used to store one alphabetical character, symbolic character, or two decimal digits. Memory and disk storage are typically measured in bytes.

Cache   A portion of memory you set up to hold data that is read from or waiting to be written to disk. Since accessing data from RAM is faster than from a disk, using a cache will speed up program execution.

CAD   Computer Aided Design. Specialized computers and application programs, used in design-related fields such as architecture, engineering, and graphic design. CAD applications are graphics and mathematics intensive, requiring fast microprocessors and high - resolution video displays.

Calculation   The performance of various mathematical operations yielding a numeric result.

Call Back   A procedure established for identifying a terminal dialing into a computer system by disconnecting the calling terminal and re-establishing the connection by having the computer system dial the telephone number of the calling terminal.

Category I   Criteria utilized in determining the classification of this area are extremely high financial impact to the enterprise, extremely high replacement value of IT systems (hardware and software), designated immediate to one-day critical application, extremely high impact to the enterprise customers, and significant regulatory reporting requirement.

Category II   Criteria utilized in determining the classification of this area are high financial impact to the enterprise, high replacement value of IT systems (hardware and software), designated two-day critical application high impact to the enterprise customers, and significant regulatory reporting requirement.

Category III Criteria utilized in determining the classification of this area are medium financial impact to the enterprise, medium replacement value of IT systems (hardware and software), designated seven-day to 10-day critical application, and medium impact to the enterprise customers.

Category IV   Criteria utilized in determining the classification of this area are low
(Client Server   financial impact to the enterprise, low replacement value of client server
Processing Area) and IT system (hardware and software), recover as soon as is practical, low impact to the enterprise customers, and area customers must access to conduct business with the enterprise.

CCTV   Closed Circuit Television

Central   CPU - A unit of a computer that includes the circuits controlling the
Processing Unit   interpretation and execution of instructions.
(CPU)

Centralized Network	Also called a server-based network. In a centralized network, data is processed at individual workstations but stored on a central, or dedicated file server (See File Server.) Centralized networks are typically larger, more powerful, and more expensive per unit than distributed networks.
Character	A unit of information that is usually composed of six, seven, or eight bits. Also, the figure that designates each unit of information.
Character Set	The group of characters a computer can recognize and process. PC-compatible computers use an extended ASCII character set.
CICS	Customer Information Control System - IBM Program Product
Cipher System	A cryptographic system in which cryptography is applied to clear text elements of equal length.
Ciphertext	Unintelligible text or signals produced through the use of cipher systems.

Client Server Access Control Zones	There are two types:
	- Public areas
	- Controlled areas (There are two types of controlled areas)
	   - General areas
	   - Restricted areas

Client Server Processing Area	Area where client server and IT occurs, assigned one of the four classifications I through IV.
Client Server Security Representative	CSSR - The primary contact for the Client Server Resource Group, responsible for ensuring that security requirements are being followed.
Clipboard	Temporary holding place that facilitates the cutting and pasting of text and graphics.
Closed Circuit Television	CCTV
Cluster	A block on all (hard) disks where data is stored.
Coaxial Cable	A connecting cable consisting of two insulating layers and two conductors. A central conductor wire is surrounded by the first layer of insulation. An outer shielding conductor is laid over this insulation and then covered with the second layer of insulation.
COBOL	(Common Business Oriented Language) A standardized code for programming a computer.
Code	A system of symbols for representing data and instructions for a computer.

Cold Boot	To reload a computer's operating system by turning the computer's power off and then back on. (If a computer has a reset switch, a cold boot can be performed without turning the power off and on.) See also Boot.
COM	File extension for a file that is executable from DOS level.
Command	An instruction, entered by a user, that tells the computer to perform a specific task.
Command Buffer	A segment of memory used to temporarily store commands. The command buffer only holds a copy of the last command issued.
Commands	System control statements which cause specific functions to be initiated, and which may be considered privileged according to their function.
Communications	The process of sending data between electronic devices.
Communications Security	The protection that ensures the authenticity of telecommunications and that results from the application of measures taken to deny unauthorized persons information of value which might be derived from accessing telecommunications.
Communications Software	The interface between the modem and PC. This software provides a means for you to send instructions to the modem from either menus or a set of commands you type in at the prompt.
Computer Resource	The aggregate of all computer generated data, programs, systems, communication facilities, and hardware. This includes, but is not limited to, PCs, mini-computers, mainframe computer systems, computer files, hard copy printouts, computer tape, computer disks, CRT terminals, and purchased or developed software.
Confidential Information	One class of sensitive information (with extremely high impact to the enterprise if disclosed) concerned with such activities as strategic planning, product development, marketing strategy, financial forecasts and results. All information addressing vulnerabilities within the enterprise, such as audits and security incident reports, is considered confidential.
Confidentiality Agreement	A statement of the user's understanding of their individual responsibilities as a system user and their knowledge that violation of security procedures is unacceptable.
Configuration Hardware	The arrangement of disk drives, memory, and peripherals which constitutes a particular PC or network node.
Configuration Software	The procedure that prepares software programs to run on the computer's specific hardware, operating system, memory capacity, peripherals, etc.
Connection Number	A number assigned to any station that attaches to a file server; it may be a different number each time a station attaches. The file server's operating system uses connection numbers to control each station's communication with other stations.

Connectivity   The ability of electronic devices to communicate (transfer data).

Console   The monitor and keyboard from which you actually view and control
                      server activity. At the console, you can type in commands to control
                      printers and disk drives, send messages, set the file server clock, shut down
                      the file server, and view file server information.

Controllability   The ability of a system to accommodate and enforce logical access
                      restrictions. Control should be exercised according to the principle of least
                      privilege.

Controlled Areas One area of client server access control zones. There are two types of
                      controlled areas:
                      - General areas
                      - Restricted areas

**Cost/Benefit   Performance of a cost-versus-loss analysis. The cost of the safeguard
Analysis**   procurement, development, installation and maintenance is compared
                      against the calculated loss should the vulnerability be allowed to remain
                      with the possibility of occurrence or exploitation.

Countermeasure   The employment of devices, methods and techniques for the purpose of
                      correcting a security weakness and blocking actualization of a threat.

CPU   See Central Processing Unit.

Crash   A slang term that means hardware or software has stopped working
                      properly (i.e. the computer fails to respond to user input).

**Critical   Applications which would cause business disruption and/or loss if the
Applications**   ability to process them as scheduled was partially or completely lost.
                      Criticality should be determined based upon collective impact of
                      processing delays or disruptions. These delays or disruptions should be
                      stated in terms of direct business impact, additional processing expenses,
                      revenue lost or enterprise embarrassment.

Criticality   The relative measure of impact on the enterprise by inadvertent or
                      deliberate disclosure (i.e., loss of privacy and/or confidentiality), alteration,
                      destruction or non-availability of that resource.

Cryptography   The art or science concerning the principles, means and methods for
                      rendering clear text unintelligible and for converting encrypted messages
                      into intelligible form.

Current Directory The directory you are working in; your default directory.

Current Drive   See Default Drive.

Cursor   Indicator of the position on a screen at which the next character keyed-in
                      will appear.

Custodian	A manager with the authority to grant access to an owned computer resource, (e.g. an application system or file).
Customer Information Control System	CICS - A general purpose data base/data communications system.
Cylinder	A set of tracks at a specific position on a platter that can be accessed simultaneously by the heads.
Data	An information resource in machine-readable and system-processable form, upon which system operations or processes are performed. Data may be single elements or aggregated into fields, records, files or data bases. Data may be of two types: system or application. The type depends upon whether it supports system control or application processing functions. Within each of these categories of data exist two additional sub-categories - production - test
Data Security System	The software running within the computer systems that control access to computer resources on PCs, mini-computers, or mainframe computer systems.
Data Classification	The assignment of a security category to an information asset, based on a sensitivity evaluation. Categories include Public, Internal Use Only, and Confidential.
Data Encryption Standard	DES - The encryption algorithm approved by NBS.
Data Language/I	DL/I - A hierarchical data base management system used by IMS or DB/2 or CICS.
Data Level 1	Confidential information for internal use only.
Data Level 2	Restricted information for internal use only.
Data Level 3	Internal use only information.
Data Level 4	Unclassified information.
Data Storage	Storage of transactions or records so that they may be retrieved upon request.
Database	An integrated file containing multiple record types or segments that may be accessed in a non-sequential manner. On a network, a collection of data organized and stored on disk by network users, usually through use of a special application program.
Debug	To identify and to eliminate faults in computer program logic or equipment.

Decipher   To convert, by use of the appropriate key, enciphered text into its
                      equivalent clear text.

Decision Table   A table listing all the conditions that may exist and the corresponding
                      actions to be performed. It permits complex logic to be expressed in a
                      concise format and may be used in lieu of flowcharts.

Decrypt   To convert, by use of the appropriate key, encrypted (encoded or
                      enciphered) text into its equivalent clear text.

Dedicated File   See File Server.
Server

Default   A value or option that is chosen automatically when no other value is
                      specified. For example, if a word processing program has a preset page
                      length, it is called the default page length.

Default Drive   The drive that a workstation is currently using. The drive prompt (A, C,
                      etc.) identifies the default drive letter.

Default Server   The file server to which your default drive is mapped. In other words, the
                      drive you are currently using is mapped to a particular file server;
                      therefore, that file server is your default server. Any commands that you
                      enter will be directed automatically to the default server unless you specify
                      otherwise.

DES   Data Encryption Standard

Descender   Portion of the lowercase letters g, j, p, q, and y that extend below the
                      baseline.

Desk Accessory   Also known as DA, a Macintosh utility that can be used while another
                      application is in use, such as a calculator or thesaurus. DAs are found
                      under the Mac's Apple menu.

Desktop   Use of PCs and software applications to produce publication-quality
Publishing   documents.

Destination   The network station, directory, drive, printer, file, etc., to which data is
                      sent.

Dialog Box   Box that appears on-screen requesting user input.

Digitizer   Device used to convert an image to a series of dots that can be read, stored,
                      and manipulated by the computer. A digitizer often scans video input,
                      while a scanner usually scans hard copy input.

Directory   A group of data files and programs on a disk. Most computers allow you
                      to separate files into directories. This simplifies finding them and speeds
                      access.

Directory Name (path)	A name that both identifies a directory and reflects its position with a directory structure. On a network, the full directory name lists the name of the file server, the volume, and each sub-directory leading down to the directory you need to access. The directory name is also called the directory path.
Directory Right	Restrictions specific to a directory that regulate trustee activity within it. Directory rights are limited to a single directory and do not extend down through the directory structure. See also maximum rights mask.
Disk	The medium used for electronic storage of computer data, similar in appearance and performance to a phonograph record. Disk drives are the machinery that read and write data on disks. Floppy disks are flexible media that are easily inserted into and removed from the computer, while hard disks are usually permanently mounted in the computer or in a accessory drive.
Disk Controller	A device, typically a circuit card in a PC, that provides the interface between a disk and the central processing unit. For example a SCSI card is both a disk controller and a controller for other SCSI devices.
Disk Drive	A storage device that allows users to read, write, and delete data. A disk drive can be internal (built into the computer) or external (attached as a peripheral to the computer). The operation of the disk drive is regulated by a disk controller.
Disk Operating System (DOS)	See DOS.
Disk Subsystem	An external unit that attaches to the file server and may contain hard disk drives, a tape drive, or both. The disk subsystem gives the file server more storage capacity.
Diskette	A flexible plastic disk (synonymous with floppy disk) in various sizes, coated with magnetic oxide and used for storing information.
Distributed Network	Also called a peer-to-peer network. In a distributed network, the file server can also be used as an individual workstation. Distributed networks are less powerful than centralized networks but are less expensive per unit and easier to install than centralized networks.
Distributed Processing	Distributing IT to several computers rather than one computer.
DL/I	Data Language/I

Documentation	The orderly presentation, organization and communication of recorded special knowledge to produce a historical record of:
	    - system objectives
	    - employed methodologies
	    - outputs
	    - responsible staff members
	    - supervisory review information
	    - training material
	    - accounting controls
	    - computer operating instruction
	Documentation can be in either printed or outline form.

DOS	(Disk Operating System) The operating system controls the movement of information in the computer. It controls the way the computer uses programs and applications.
Dot-matrix	A method of generating characters with a matrix of dots.
Download	The act of transferring files from one computer to another or of loading fonts from a computer to a printer.
Downloading	Receiving data from another PC.
DPI	(Dots Per Inch) A measure of a printer's or video monitor's resolution. A laser printer's resolution is 300 dpi. Most monitors are around 72dpi.
DRAM	Dynamic RAM. A type of random access memory that stores information for only a short period of time. (Compare with Static Ram - SRAM).
Drive Letter	A letter that can represent a local drive, a network drive, or a logical drive.
Drive Mapping	A layout of the identifiers associated with each disk drive and its files.
Drop Crop	First letter of a paragraph set in a larger point size than the rest of the text, and inset into the text block.
Dummy	A guide produced prior to layout of a publication that shows the position of text, artwork, and advertising.
E-mail	Messages exchanged among computer used on a network.
EBCDIC	(Extended Binary Coded Decimal Interchange Code) A character code used by IBM's larger computers.
Edit	A general control term that includes format check, completeness check, check digits, reasonableness tests, limit check, validity check, etc. Generally implies implementation via a computer program.

Effective Rights   The rights a user may actually exercise in a given directory. Two factors determine effective rights: (1) trustee rights granted to a particular user; (2) directory rights specified in the directory's maximum rights mask. Since directory rights always take precedence over trustee rights, any trustee right not specifically denied in the maximum rights mask is an effective right.

EGA   Display screen technology that provides 640 x 350 dots on the screen. This is obsolete technology and was replaced by VGA and super VGA.

EISA   Enhanced Industry Standard Architecture. Several PC manufacturers banded together to design a bus that extends the ISA 8- and 16- bit bus design to 32 bits. One advantage of buying a 386 PC with an EISA bus architecture is its downward compatibility; your existing 8- bit and 16- bit boards can fit into EISA 32- bit slots.

Electronic Mail   See E-Mail.

En   Typographic unit of measure equaling one-half the width of the em space, approximately the width of the letter "n" of the particular typeface in use.

Encipher   To convert clear text into an unintelligible form by means of a cipher system.

Encryption   Transforms understandable information (clear text) into a form which is not intelligible (ciphertext) unless one has knowledge of the key used to perform the transformation. Used to protect sensitive information from disclosure and to make it extremely difficult to fraudulently modify information.

Enhancement   An enhancement request is defined as a change, modification, or redesign of programs in production, test, or development. It also refers to the creation of new functionality or an entirely new application.

EOJ   End of Job.

EPS   (Encapsulated PostScript); a document file format jointly developed by Aldus, Adobe, and Altsys to facilitate the exchange of PostScript graphics files between applications.

EXE   File extension for a file that is executable from DOS level.

Expanded Memory   Memory outside the DOS 1MB limit that is accessed in revolving blocks. Because expanded memory was developed to respond to the 8088's memory limitations, it is only available on add-in boards.

Exposure Analysis   That element of the overall risk management process that deals with the estimation of the probable loss in the event of an undesirable occurrence.

Extended Memory   In a PC running DOS, extended memory is memory above the 1MB address range. Normally, this memory is available to DOS only as a virtual disk (memory that is treated as though it were a disk drive).

External Icons   Icons from non-Windows applications or ones you create.

External Modem   External modems sit next to a PC. It connects to the PC through one of the serial ports located on the back of the PC.

FAT   (File Allocation Table) A table that helps the operating system keep track of where particular files are located.

Field   An element of data within a record that constitutes an item of information. Example: name, account number, amount.

File   A program or collection of related information. Each set of information or document stored on a computer is typically kept in a separate file on a disk or diskette.

File Attributes   Designations that regulate how a file may be handled on the network. For example, a file can be assigned the attributes "Shareable" and "Read/Only." "Shareable" means that more than one user may access the file at the same time; "Read/Only" means that users can read the file, but they cannot alter it.

File Maintenance   Changing information in a file through addition, deletion, or replacement usually to information that will have a sustained impact on future processing.

File Server   A PC that contains the network's shared resources and serves as a remote hard drive for any PCs that are attached to it. Centralized networks use dedicated servers - PCs that are used only as file servers. (See Centralized Network and Distributed Network.)

File Sharing   An important feature of networking that allows more than one user to access the same file at the same time. See also multi-user network; file attributes.

File Transfer Protocol   FTP for short, is the main Internet technology for locating and downloading files from a server.

Fix   A fix is defined as a program that is currently in production that has a problem; it is not working the way that it is should.

Flash left/right   Lines of text that are aligned vertically along the left/right margin leaving the opposite edge ragged.

Flat-File Database   The simplest type of database. Flat-file databases are so named because you can only maintain one file at a time. (Compare with relational database.)

Floating-Point   A method of storing numeric calculations where the decimal point is not in a fixed location.

Floppy Disk Drive	A disk drive that reads from and writes to a floppy diskette.
Floppy Diskette	Another name for a flexible diskette, a removable magnetic storage medium.
Flowchart	A diagram that presents through symbols and connecting lines either the logical structure of a computer program or the sequence of processes in a system.
Folio	Page number or other information that appears at the top or bottom of a page throughout a publication.
Font	An assortment or set of type faces all of one size and style (e.g. 10 pt. Courier, 14 pt. Times Roman, 6 pt. Helvetica, etc.).
FORMAT (noun)	The logical or physical arrangement of the tracks and sectors on a floppy diskette or a hard disk.

FORMAT (verb)	An operating system function that prepares a disk so that it can store data.
	    1/4 Double Density Mini-floppy (obsolete)
	    360 K5 1/4 High Density Mini-floppy (obsolete)
	    1.2 MB 3 1/2 Double Density Micro-floppy
	    720 K3 1/2 High Density Micro-floppy (obsolete)
	    1.44 MB 3½" Diskette

FTP	See File Transfer Protocol.
Gallery	A typeset and formatted draft used for proofreading copy and estimating article length.
General Areas	One of the types of controlled areas within Client Server Access Control Zones. Areas of enterprise property or activity accessed by the enterprise staff members, agents acting on behalf of the enterprise or others designated by appropriate authorities as requiring access.
Gigabyte	One billion bytes.
Gopher	Gopher is a system of menus that can lead you to information that is wanted on the Internet.
Graphical Format	Various computer formats for creating and storing images (see bit-mapped, objected-oriented, and PostScript as examples).
Graphical User Interface	An operating system that communicates computer data largely through the manipulation of graphic images on the computer screen (as distinguished from the command language of DOS, above).
Graphics	Pictures, graphs or other images. Different combinations of hardware and software may have different capabilities for creating and processing graphics.

Graphics Application   Software used to create and manipulate pictures and other images. Types include painting, drawing, and charting packages, commonly used in homes and offices, as well as computer-assisted design (CAD) and computer-assisted mechanics (CAM), used in manufacturing and other industries.

Grid   A page template containing predefined margins and columns.

Group Access   A method of granting identical rights to several users at the same time so they can all access the same directories. Rather than repetitively assigning each individual user the same rights, the network supervisor can make each user a member of the same group, then grant that group the needed rights.

GUI   (Graphical User Interface) A new technology for IBM PC and clones. Microsoft Windows is a GUI. Many PC applications are bring developed using GUI as opposed to a character-based user interface. Apple's Macintosh uses a GUI which has been used since the Macintosh was introduced.

Gutter   Inner margin of a page that makes an allowance for binding.

Hard Copy   Printed reports, listings, etc., produced by a computer on paper.

Hard Disk   A magnetic disk made of rigid material, which is non-removable or sealed. The type of hard disks installed in PCs use Winchester technology, and are also referred to as Winchester Disks.
Note - Approx. storage size equivalents:
      3 ½ inch diskette 180 pages or 10 megabytes 5,000 pages
      3 ½ inch laser disk 200,000 pages

Hard Disk Interleave   A system for minimizing the time to read consecutive sectors from a single track of the hard disk. In a 1-to-1 interleave, the sectors are numbered consecutively. In a 2-to-1 interleave, every other sector is numbered consecutively.

Hardware   The physical, tangible, and permanent components of a computer or data-processing system.

Hayes Compatibility   A standard command set that links communications software to the modem. This command set was first developed by Hayes Microcomputer Products, Inc.

Head   The electromagnetic mechanism in a disk drive that writes data to and retrieves data from an electronic medium (platters).

HERTZ (Hz)   A unit of frequency equal to one cycle per second.

Hierarchy   Refers to a directory structure made up of different levels in which some directories are parts of others and the entire structure is organized in a branching, tree-like form.

High Level Format	The process, after a low level format is completed, that creates the directory structure and file allocation tables (FAT) needed by DOS. This type of format is what most computer users view as a regular DOS format. That is, formatting a disk using FORMAT.COM (included with DOS) is a high level format.
Home Directory	A network directory that the network supervisor creates specifically for you. The supervisor may include a drive mapping to your home directory in your log-on script.
Home Page	A page on a WWW site that describes some entity on the Internet.
Host	A computer, attached to a network, that provides services to another computer beyond simply storing and forwarding information. Mainframes, minicomputers, and file servers are sometimes called hosts, but the term is often used more broadly. For example, the network station that a remote caller takes over and controls is referred to as a host.
HyperCard	Software designed to manage data and control other application software through "hypertext" technology.
Hypertext	A computer information technology that allows data and/or software to be arranged in any sequence, not just in linear order like ordinary words on a page.
I/O	Abbreviation for Input/Output.
IBM PC Compatible	A computer that can run the software written for the IBM PC and use the expansion devices designed for the IBM PC. Not all machines called compatible are completely compatible.
Icon	Small image that graphically represents an object, concept, function, or message on the computer screen.
Identification	The process whereby an individual requests use of or access to a controlled resource and claims an identity. Level of identification and frequency of requests to provide identification are determined by the sensitivity of the information and the criticality of the process.
IEEE	Institute for Electrical and Electronic Engineers.
IMS or DB/2	Information Management System or Data Base/2 - IBM product.
Inadvertent Disclosure	Accidental exposure of sensitive information to a person not having authorized access. This may result in a compromise or a need-to-know violation.
Individual Accountability	Measures to positively associate the identity of a user with his access to machines, material, and the time, method and degrees of access.
Information Integrity	The state that exists when computerized information is the same as that in the source documents and has not been exposed to accidental or malicious alteration or destruction.

Information Management System	IMS or DB/2 - A general purpose data base/data communications system.
Information Security	The protection of information from accidental, unauthorized, intentional, or malicious modification, destruction, or disclosure.
Information Support Managers	The manager responsible for the operating integrity of an information system. This manager must be of vice president level or above and is responsible for requesting appropriate establishment or modification to the access control restrictions for an information system resource. This request requires approval of the owner of that resource.
Information Technology Security Committee	An official committee of the enterprise which establishes policy on matters relating to the security and privacy of customer, employee and enterprise information.
Initial Program Load	IPL - Process used to load and start the operating system into a computer. The same as "Booting up a computer"
Input	Data to be transferred to the computer.
Integrity	The assurance that a system or a process should perform its designed function in an accurate and consistent manner.
Inter Network	(Internet) Two or more networks connected by an internal or external bridge. Users on an inter-network may use the resources (files, disk drives, etc.) of all connected networks. See also Bridge.
Interface	The way in which the parts of a computer - or the computer and its user - communicate with each other.
Interleave	The staggered spacing of consecutive sectors around the tracks of a disk. Typically expressed as a ratio, to account for the rapid rotation of the platters. An optimal interleave spaces sectors to maximize disk performance.
Internal Modem	Internal modems come on a card which is inserted inside the PC.
Internal Use Information	One class of sensitive information (with medium impact to the enterprise if disclosed) commonly shared within the company, including operating procedures, policies, interoffice memorandums and the internal directory.
Internet	A public access network which links most universities, government agencies and commercial enterprises.
Intranet	A private access network which links based on Internet protocols.
IPL	Initial Program Load. See also Boot.
IPX	Inter-network Packet Exchange, a protocol that allows the exchange of message packets on an inter-network.

ISA	Industry Standard Architecture. IBM's original bus design found in XTs, ATs, and their compatibles. The ISA bus comes in two versions: an 8- bit bus and a 16- bit bus. This is obsolete technology.
ISO	International Standards Organization.
Jaggie	Unwanted jagged edges produced by lower-resolution printers or images.
JCL	(Job Control Language) A language used by programmers to give the computer operating system the specifications and instructions for a job.
Job Function	The duties and actions required of an employee to perform his/her job.
Justified Text	Lines of type that are aligned at both the left and right edges.
KB	Abbreviation for "kilobytes," one KB equals 1024 bytes.
Kern	In typesetting, adjusting the space between characters so that they are closer than standard allowance.
Key	In cryptography, a sequence of symbols that controls the operations of encryption and decryption.
Key Generation	The origination of a key or of a set of distinct keys.
Kilobyte	One thousand bytes.
Labeling	The external or internal identification of transaction batches or files according to source, application, date, or other identifying characteristics.
LAN	See Local Area Network.
LAN Bridge	A software and hardware connection between two networks, usually of similar design. For example, a PC with two LAN adapters which allows two local LANs to logically function as one LAN. If a bridge is located in a file server, it is an internal bridge. If a bridge is located in a workstation, it is an external bridge. Most LAN bridges are dedicated, although some bridges can also function as servers. LAN bridges can be used to "bridge" dissimilar topologies. This allows joining LANs from different vendors such as IBM (token ring), Apple (Apple Net), and Ethernet. See also Inter-Network.
LAN Gateway	A PC which is physically and logically connected to two remote LANs. A PC on the LAN can "pass through the gate" and access the other remote LAN.
LAN Host Gateway	A control unit which is physically and logically connected to the LAN and a host computer. A PC on the LAN can "pass through the gate" and access the host computer.
Laser	High speed printer that produces letter-quality hard copy of computer data using laser technology.

Leading	Pronounced ledor. Additional white space between lines of type. In hot type, this is done by adding non-printing strips of lead between lines of type.
Leased Equipment	Leased equipment is that equipment which the enterprise has indirect title to, is not being depreciated and is maintained at the expense of the enterprise. This includes equipment on the premises of the enterprise, its customers, its agents and its employees.
Least Privilege	The principle which states that individuals should be given only that level of authority and granted only those privileges and accesses necessary to successfully accomplish their assigned duties. Individuals should not be allowed either functional or physical access to controlled areas or operations unless required by their duties and requested by their supervisor.
Letter-Quality	A measure of comparing print quality to that of good typewriters. (i.e. Daisy wheel).
Levels Of Access Authority	Specific levels of access authority established for each controlled area. There are two general levels of access authority: - Permanent Access - Temporary Access
Library Routine	A standard set of program instructions maintained in on-line storage that may be called in and processed by other programs.
Line art	Black-and-white illustration containing no gray tones.
Local Area Network (LAN)	A linked group of computers and peripheral devices. The computers may share the peripheral devices and transfer information easily from computer to perform necessary business or system functions.
Local Disk	A disk that is attached to a workstation but is not part of the network. A local disk can be accessed only by the workstation to which it is attached. It does not contain network files and cannot be accessed by other stations on the network.
Log	A record on paper or machine-readable media of all transactions, operating instructions, etc., sequenced in the order they occurred.
LOG-OFF (Verb)	The process of properly exiting the local area network through the use of a specific log off command (i.e., LOG OFF). Generally, the workstation then reverts to a stand-alone PC and the user may only access local peripherals.
LOG-ON (Noun)	The process of accessing the network.
LOG-ON (Verb)	To gain access to the network. Logging in to the network involves executing a log-on script and establishing yourself as a user.
Log-On Id	A unique code that identifies a user to the computer system.

Low Level Format	The preliminary process that establishes track and sector areas on the platters of a drive so the drive can locate data. Normally this process destroys all data, but some disk maintenance programs can perform a non-destructive low level format. There are a few PC low-level formatting packages. Hard disks are usually sold already low-level formatted. Users must run FDISK after a low level format, whereas with a high level format, it is unnecessary.
LU	(Logical Unit) These can represent end users, application programs, or other devices (contrast with physical units).
Macro	A "program" to carry out tasks or calculations. Macros save you time by "remembering" the keystrokes for the command sequences and calculations you use frequently and carrying them out when you need them.
Mainframe	A large, very powerful computer typically operated by a full-time staff of IT professionals. It may be used to provide computing to many users or to perform a few tasks that require a great deal of processing, such as check processing.
Mask	A technique used in graphics programs that make use of an opaque image to block out an area of an illustration.
Master File	A computer file containing information to be retained and reused for reference or in file maintenance. Contrast with transaction file.
Master Page	A feature established in many page-layout programs that allows the user to specify text and graphic elements that will appear on every page of the publication.
Math Co-Processor	A specialized computer chip that can be added onto your PC's main board (motherboard). A math co-processor helps the CPU perform complex mathematical calculations.
MB	Abbreviation for "Megabytes," or "millions of bytes."
MBPS	Megabits per second (one million bits per second).
MCA	Micro Channel Architecture. IBM's newest generation of bus design introduced with the PS/2. It is a 32- bit bus (low-end PS/2s have a 16- bit MCA bus) designed to allow more than one CPU in a single machine.
Megabyte	One million bytes.
MEGAHERTZ - (MHz)	A measure of frequency 1,000,000 hertz. This is used to measure the processing speed of a computer chip.
Memory	(Synonymous with storage) The section of a computer system or any device in which data and programmable information can be inserted and stored.

Memory Board	An add-on board designed to increase the amount of random access memory within a PC.
Memory Interleaving	Another method (caching is the other alternative) for speeding access to the computer's memory. RAM is divided into two banks or pages which enables the microprocessor to access one bank while the other is being refreshed.
Merge	To combine two files into one.
Microprocessor	A microchip containing integrated circuits that execute instructions (for example, 8086, 8087, 80286, 80386, 80486, and so on).
MIPS	Million instructions per second.
Modem	A hardware device that transmits and receives data via telephone lines from one computer device to another or to a network resource, such as a file server.
Moiré	Undesirable pattern created when halftone screens are improperly aligned.
Monitor	A term for the display screen attached to a processing unit or workstation.
Mouse	Small hand held pointing device which you move around on a flat surface in order to position the cursor on a video display.
MSNF	Multiple Systems Network Facility
Multi-Finder	A component of Macintosh System software that allows the user to run two or more applications at once.
Multi-Server Network	A single network that has two or more file servers operating on it. On a multi-server network, users may access files from any file server to which they are attached (if they have access rights). A multi-server network should not be confused with an inter-network (two or more networks linked together through a bridge).
Multi-Station Access Units (MSAU)	Physically connects LAN components to the LAN wire.
Multi-Tasking	System in which a computer can run two or more programs at the same time. Apple's Multi-finder and IBM's OS/2 are multitasking operating systems. By contrast, MS-DOS is a single tasking operating system.
Multi-User	A system that can be used by more than one person at the same time.
Multi-User Network	An operation system that allows several users (at separate workstations) to share a system's resources, such as processing power, data, printers, disks, etc.

Multiple Systems Network Facility	MSNF - A VTAM (Virtual Telecommunications Access Method) application whose purpose is to allow a terminal access to multiple systems without the use of multiple cabling.
Multiple Virtual Storage	MVS- The operating system used on large IBM mainframe computers.
MVS	Multiple Virtual Storage
National Bureau Of Standards	NBS
National Fire Protection Association	NFPA
NBS	National Bureau of Standards
Need-To-Know	The necessity for access to, knowledge of, or possession of sensitive information in order to carry out assigned duties. Responsibility for determining whether a person's duties require possession or access to certain information, and whether that person is authorized to receive it, rests upon the individual having current possession, knowledge or control of the information involved (e.g., the owner) and not upon the prospective recipient.
Network	See Local Area Network (LAN).
Network Communication-	Data transmission between network stations. Requests for services and data are passed from one network station to another through a communication medium such as cabling.
Network Components	Controllers, concentrators, modems, protocol converters and network software.
Network Interface Card (NIC)	An add-on board that is installed in a PC's expansion slot, allowing it to communicate as part of a local-area network.
Network Operation	A user given special responsibilities on the network. For example, a print queue operator is a user who is allowed to manage printer queues, changing the position of jobs in the queue or deleting them altogether.
Network Station	Any PC (or other device) connected to a network by means of a network interface board and some communication medium. A network station can be a workstation, bridge, or server.
NFPA	National Fire Protection Association
Nibble	Any combination of four bits. For example, 0110 is a nibble. A nibble is sometimes called a half-byte.

Node	An individual device on the network. Although "node" most commonly refers to PCs, a node can also be a printer or any other device.
Non sensitive Information	Information designated to be available for public use, such as published annual reports, marketing material, branch programs, etc.
NT	A high end 32 bit windows based operating systems.
NTFS	(NT file System) A disk recording system for NT systems which allows for long file names. It is intended for larger disk drives and is more reliable than FAT.
Object-Oriented Graphic	Graphic images formed with continuous geometric shapes; the software used to produce these graphics is often referred to a draw-type software.
OCR	(Optical Character Recognition) A method of scanning typewritten, printed, or handwritten documents, and translating the data into editable text.
Off-Line	Equipment, devices, or files not electronically connected to a computer.
On-Line	Equipment, devices, or files that are electronically connected to a computer for purposes of access.
Operating Data	All information that passes into or out of a department, or may be subject to inquiry from outside the department.
Operating System	Software procedures that tell the computer how to operate programs. MS-DOS and UNIX are two examples of operating systems.
Operational	An operational is defined as a system change needed to reduce processing risks, to improve system availability, to increase operational efficiency, or enhance system controls and integrity.
Optimize	To make all files on a disk "continuous," or physically linked together on a (hard) drive.
Orphan	A single word or part of a word from the last line of a paragraph that appears at the top of a column.
Output	Results of computer processing.
Owners	All information system resources should be assigned to an owner, not implying full rights of ownership (i.e., the enterprise retains the rights to authorize the sale, distribution or destruction of a resource). The owner is the end-user or person responsible for the assets controlled by a system.

Parallel Interface	A means of transmitting data from the computer to a printer. To do so, the computer must be equipped with a parallel interface, also known as a parallel port. (e.g. LPT1:, LPT2:)
Parking	Positioning the read/write heads away from the active use areas of a disk to rest over either a less used area or a "safe zone" that has been marked as unusable for data storage; it precludes the possibility of physical and magnetic damage when the system is powered up or powered down.
Partition	A portion of a hard disk's physical storage space that is allocated to an operating system (DOS, etc.). Once created, a partition belongs exclusively to the specified operating system; no other operating system can access that area. A subdivision (created with FDISK) that can be used to split a disk into more than one logical drive (C: and D:) or to run an alternate operating system. It must be established after a low level format and before a high level format.
Password	A protected word or a string of characters that identifies or authenticates a user.
Password	A secret code entered at log-on time to verify the identity of the person attempting to use an individual Log-on ID.
Password Protection	A security feature that requires a user to enter a correct password before being allowed to log in to the network.
Path	Directories that are to be searched by the operating system when the name of the program a user wants to execute is typed. If the program isn't found in the current sub-directory, the path will be searched until either a program by that name is found or the end of the search path is reached. To define the path, type "path=" at the DOS prompt, followed by all of the sub-directory names that are to be searched, separating them with semi-colons. For example: path C:\;C:\WORD;C:\CHART;C:\PROJ See your DOS manual for more information.
PCF	Programmed Cryptographic Facility
PDL	(Page Description Language) Computer code that tells a printer where to mark a page.
Peripheral Equipment	A device other than the main computer that can enhance its capabilities. Peripherals include printers, modems, disk drives, tape drives, monitors, keyboards, scanners, and plotters.

Permanent Access	Permanent staff members who have responsibility for functions performed in a controlled area may be granted permanent access privileges to that area. Permanent access privileges should not be granted to staff members who do not work in controlled areas or do not enter controlled areas on a frequent basis. Temporary staff members who function in a position in a controlled area more than 30 days may be granted permanent access privileges if requested by the manager with administrative responsibility for that temporary staff member.
Personal Identification Number	PIN - A code used for the identification of an individual.
Personnel Security	The procedures established to ensure that all personnel who have access to any sensitive information have the required authorities as well as all appropriate clearances.
Physical Security	The use of locks, guards, badges and similar measures to control access to the computer and related equipment. The measures required for the protection of the structures housing the computer, related equipment and their contents from damage by accident, fire and environmental hazards.
Pica	Printer's unit of measurement used principally in typesetting. One pica equals approximately 1/6 of an inch.
Pict	Standard format used for object-oriented graphics on the Macintosh.
PIN	Personal Identification Number
Pitch	The number of characters printed per horizontal inch.
Pixel	Short for picture element, a dot of light that illuminates a monitor. The number of pixels in a given space is a measure of picture resolution.
Platter	The physical medium, or surface, onto which data is magnetically recorded and read back.
Point	Standard unit of typographic measurement from the top of the ascender to the bottom of the descended. There are approximately 72 points to an inch.
PORT (Verb)	To move from one environment to another.
Postscript	A computer language developed by Adobe Systems, Inc., to describe computerized page layouts for a computer printer. PostScript fonts, which store characters as outlines to allow sophisticated changes in type size, has become the most common standard for desktop publishing. Some graphics software uses a special encapsulated PostScript (EPS) format that takes advantage of this language.
Print	A DOS command that lets you print text files and also customize the way your system handles printing tasks.

Print Buffer	A segment of memory used to temporarily store data as it is transferred from the PC to the printer.
Print Device	A printer, plotter, or other peripheral used to create hard copy.
Print Queue	A "waiting line" to have printing done on a particular printer. See also Queue.
Print Server	A PC with printers accessed by the LAN.
Print Spooling	A multi-tasking operation wherein a program that controls output to a printer runs as a background operation. Print spooling allows you to send files to your printer and to continue working with your computer even as the files are printing.
Printer	A device that produces a hard copy (e.g. paper) of the information displayed on a computer screen (or in a file).
Printer's Error	Typographical error made by typesetter. Abbreviated as 'P.E.'
Privacy	The right of individuals and organizations to control the collection, storage, and dissemination of their information or information about themselves.
Process Printing	The printing from a series of two or more halftone plates to produce intermediate colors and shades.
Production Data	Production data is used to support versions of systems or application software which have been approved for production or live operations.
Program	A set of instructions that tells the computer how to handle a problem. A series of statements of action that achieve a specific result.
Program	An integral set of sequentially coded instructions used to control computer system activity. Programs are generally of two types: - system - application
Programmed Cryptographic Facility	PCF - An IBM program product providing the capability to encipher/decipher data within a host processor or transmitted over a data communication path.
Prompt	A character or message (from the software) that appears on the terminal screen that requires a response from the user. "D" and "Enter your password:" are examples of prompts.
Protected Mode	A mode of operation that allows programs to use extended memory. When 286s and 386s are working above DOS's 1MB limit, they are in protected mode. 8088 microprocessors cannot access protected mode. See also Real Mode.

Protocol   A set of rules that determines how devices on a LAN communicate. Networks vary in the types of protocols they use. For example, the Apple Macintosh uses the AppleTalk protocol; Novell Netware uses the IPX protocol.

PU   (Physical Unit) This represents something tangible, such as a terminal or network controller (contrast with logical units).

Public Access   A security condition that gives all users access rights to a particular system resource. For example, all users must be able to access operating system utilities. Therefore, system utilities are usually placed in a directory that has public access rights; in other words, all users have the right to open, read, and search for files in that directory.

Public Areas   Areas of enterprise property or activity to which the general public has unlimited access (e.g., retail enterprise offices, office lobbies). Public areas should not be controlled by an access control system.

Purchased Equipment   Purchased equipment is that equipment which the enterprise has direct title to, is being depreciated and maintained at the expense of the enterprise. This includes equipment on the premises of the enterprise, its customers, its agents and its employees.

Queue   A data-handling structure that stores requests (such as print jobs) in the order they are received while they await servicing. The first request that arrives is the first to be handled. Later requests are placed in the queue and must "wait in line" to be processed unless assigned a higher priority.

RACF   Resource Access Control Facility (an IBM mainframe security system)

RAM   (Random Access Memory) Internal computer memory for programs and data that may be altered. Information in RAM will be lost if it is not saved before the computer is turned off.

Random Access   A manner of storing records in a file so that an individual record may be accessed without reading other records.

Read   To retrieve data from a storage medium. For example, when a computer transfers data from a hard disk drive into its memory, the computer is "reading" the data from the hard disk.

Read Only Files   Files that the user can access but cannot change. This is a type of data security that protects files.

Real Mode   A mode of operation in which 286 and 386 computers simulate an 8088 computer. In real mode 286 and 386 PCs are limited to 1MB of memory and cannot access extended memory. See also Protected Mode.

Reboot   See Cold Boot; Remote Reset; and Warm Boot.

Record   A set of one or more consecutive fields relating to the same subject.

Record Locking   An important feature of the network operating system that prevents different users from gaining simultaneous access to the same record in a shared file, thus preventing overlapping disk writes and ensuring data integrity.

Recover   Restore files or data to a usable condition after system failure.

Register   Positioning of elements in printing so their image will be located exactly as desired on the printed sheet or WEB; especially with reference to applying additional colors.

Relational Database   A database that lets you retrieve information from two or more files using a common field to link the files.

Remote   A connection between a LAN and a workstation or network, often using telephone lines. A remote connection (i.e. a telecommunications link) allows data to be sent and received across distances greater than those allowed by normal cabling.

Remote Job Entry   RJE - Submission of job control statements and data from a remote terminal to be executed at a host computer.

Remote Reset   A feature that enables a workstation to boot from the network, without using a local disk. See also Boot.

Remote Workstation   A terminal or PC that is not part of the local area network, but is connected to the LAN by a bridge. A remote workstation may be either a stand-alone or part of another network. It may be attached through special wiring or phone lines.

Removable Cartridge System   A high-capacity storage system that can be removed from the PC. A removable cartridge system consists of a drive mechanism and the cartridges used to store data. The most well-known removable cartridge system is the Bernoulli Box by Iomega Corp.

Reporting   Summary or exception information printed and used for management decisions or accounting entries.

Reprography   Copying and duplicating (e.g., on a high-speed photocopier).

Resource   In an information system, any function, device or information collection that may be allocated to users or programs.

Resource Access Control Facility   RACF - An IBM program product which controls users, information system resources and access authorities.

Restore   To copy data from a back-up storage device to the network or workstation.

Restricted Areas   One of the types of controlled areas within Client Server Access Control Zones. Areas of enterprise property in which sensitive or critical activities are conducted. Access is restricted to those individuals formally granted access based upon supported need.

Restricted Information	A type of sensitive information (with high impact to the enterprise if disclosed) of a personal nature about enterprise staff members or customers which the enterprise, as custodian of that information, is obligated to protect. This classification also includes production data and software. For the encryption policy, information, if disclosed or modified, that could result in unauthorized use or immediate disbursement of enterprise assets or customer or staff member assets held in trust.
RGB	Technology used to send color images from the computer to a display screen.
Rights	Privileges (assigned by the network supervisor) that control how users may work with files in a given directory (for example, controlling whether a user may read a file, change a file, or delete a file).
Risk	The probability or likelihood that a threat agent should successfully mount a specific attack against a particular system, facility or operational vulnerability.
Risk Analysis	An analysis of system assets and vulnerabilities to establish an expected loss from certain events based on estimated probabilities of occurrence of those events.
Risk Analysis Program	Designed to assist management in arriving at intelligent safeguard decisions in light of risk, loss, or embarrassment factors. Intended to complement the planning, budgeting and project management processes.
Risk Assessment	The process of evaluating threats and vulnerabilities, both known and postulated, to determine expected loss and establish the degree of acceptability to system operations.
RJE	Remote Job Entry
RJE	(Remote Job Entry) The sending of information in batch form from a remote site to an IBM mainframe.
ROM	(Read Only Memory) Part of the computer's memory used to permanently store programs whose contents can be read but not altered. ROM is usually used to store low-level operating routines.
Root Directory	The highest level in a hierarchical directory structure. It is the main directory on a network volume; all other directories are sub-directories of the root directory. Network users with sufficient rights may create sub-directories beneath a root directory. The root directory does not have a name; it is implied by the volume name (e.g. "C:\", "F:\", "SYS:").
Run	The execution of a computer program.

Satisfactory Compliance	The criteria used to determine if asset protection controls are effectively used: - proper identification and classification of assets - consistency and continuity of controls applied - timely, effective response to the attribute of auditability
Scanner	Hardware that scans (electronically reads) images and translates them into digital information for use on a computer. Scanners may be sheet fed, permitting scanning of images on single sheets of paper that are fed trough the scanner, flatbed, or hand held, permitting scanning of both paper and other objects.
Screen Printing	Formerly known as silk screen, this method employs a porous screen of fine silk, Nylon, Dacron, or stainless steel mounted on a frame. A stencil is produced on the screen in which the non-printing areas are protected by the stencil. Printing is done on paper or other substrate under the screen by applying ink with a paint-like consistency of data by a computer user. Its contents disappear when the computer is turned off.
Scroll	To move the display on a screen or in a window up, down, left, or right.
SCSI	(Small Computer System Interface) Industry standard for connecting peripheral devices to PCs; up to seven SCSI devices can be daisy-chained to a computer.
Search Drive	A drive letter assigned to a network directory in which the operating system will automatically search for an executable file (or data files accessed by the executable files) if the file is not found in the current (default) directory. A search drive allows a user working in one directory to access an application that is located in another directory.
Sectors	The smallest unit of storage on a hard disk. Typically consists of 512 bytes. Each disk track is divided into several sectors.
Secure Custody	Information assets are provided security similar to tangible assets such as cash, negotiable securities, etc.
Security	The control over users as they access and work with directories and files on a network. On most networks there are four levels of security: log-on/password security, trustee security, directory security, and file attributes security. See also Password Protection; Rights; File Attributes.
Security Equivalence	A feature of network security that allows the supervisor to quickly and easily assign one user or group the same trustee rights as another user or group.
Security Exposure	The lack of necessary controls to prevent the unauthorized use or abuse of computer resources.
Security Violation	A deliberate or accidental attempt to access, use, modify, create, destroy, or disclose computer resources in an unauthorized manner.

Sensitive Application	An application which requires protection due to the risk and magnitude of loss or harm which could result from: disclosure, alteration or destruction of data, or improper operation or deliberate manipulation of the computer application itself.
Sensitive Blank Forms	Preprinted physical media which, when filled in, become negotiable instruments or documents which authorize transfer of ownership or custody of protected enterprise resources.
Sensitive Documents	Physical media on which sensitive enterprise data is clearly and plainly displayed.
Sensitive Information	Three classes of sensitive information: - Confidential Information - Restricted Information - Internal Use Information
Separation Of Duties	A clear separation of duties so as to prevent an individual from taking advantage of the system or supporting operations. Certain functions which must be separated physically in order to reduce the possibility of an individual taking advantage of that function, to inhibit collusion and conspiracy to defraud or misappropriate resources. The same person should not initiate, authorize and enter a transaction.
Serial Interface	A means of transmitting data from the computer to a printer, modem, or other device. To have serial transmission, the computer must be equipped with a serial interface, also known as a serial port. The serial port must be initialized (e.g. COM1:, COM2).
Server	See File Server.
Shareware	Software that is freely distributed for evaluation, but requires a small fee from those who decide to keep it.
Sheet fed	Presses that print on sheets of paper rather than rolls.
Signature	A large sheet printed with four or a multiple of four pages, which, when folded, becomes a section of a publication.
Site License	A license which permits the use of proprietary software only at named locations.
SMF	System Management Facility
Software	The electronic instructions used to enter and manipulate computer data. Comprised of the following elements: - programs - commands - transactions
Sort	To arrange items or records into a sequence.

Spider   A spider is a program that automatically searches WWW pages and develops electronic indexes based on what it finds.

Spool   To transfer data that was intended for a peripheral device (such as a printer) into temporary storage. From there, the data can be transferred to the peripheral at a later time, without affecting or delaying the system as it performs other operations, SPX (Sequenced Packet Exchange) A protocol by which two workstations or applications communicate across the network. SPX uses IPX to deliver the messages, but SPX guarantees delivery of the messages and maintains the order of messages on the packet stream.

SRAM   Static RAM. A type of RAM that holds its contents as long as the power is on. DRAM, on the other hand, has to be refreshed many times a second.

Standardization Uniform, structured, and consistent procedures are developed for all processing.

Station   See Network Station.

Station Address A unique number assigned to each station on a network. It may be specified in either decimal or hexadecimal format. Also called "physical node address" or "node address."

Station Number See Connection Number.

Storage   A device or medium (floppy diskette, hard disk, magnetic tape, etc.) that receives and holds data for retrieval. Storage may be permanent or temporary.

Storage Protection A provision by the software to protect against unauthorized reading or writing between portions of storage.

Stripping   See Image Assembly.

Style Sheet   A collection of specifications used for the formatting of text such as typeface, type size, paragraph indents, and spacing.

Sub-Directory   Any directory that is below another directory in the directory structure. For example: C:\WORD\DATA; DATA is a sub-directory of WORD.

Supervisor   The network supervisor is the person responsible for the smooth operation of the whole network. (The supervisor may also install the network.) The network supervisor maintains the network, reconfiguring and updating it as the need arises. Generally, the network supervisor has all rights in all file server volumes and directories, and these rights cannot be revoked. Other users or groups may be granted a security equivalence to the network supervisor.

Supporting Utilities Power and telephone lines, air conditioning units, back-up power units, and water or fuel storage tanks supporting Client Server Processing Areas.

System Program   A program that deals with instructions that translate, load, supervise, maintain, control or otherwise perform executive or management functions for the computer.

Tape   A strip of material that may be coated or impregnated with magnetic or optically sensitive substances and used for data input, storage, or output.

TCP/IP   See Transmission Control Protocol.

Tele-Communications   Electronic communications from one computer to another via telephone lines.

Telephone Line Controller   A device that intercepts a call and determines whether it's coming from a fax, a modem, or a telephone.

Template   A publication that provides the structure and layout for corresponding publications.

Temporary Access   Permanent staff members who are not authorized to access a controlled area should only be granted temporary access privileges. Temporary staff members who will function in a position in a controlled area for less than 30 days should be granted temporary access privileges to that area. In addition, only temporary access privileges should be granted to short-term non-staff members, such as visitors, vendors, support staff members and maintenance crews.

Terminal Identification   The means used to establish the unique identification of a terminal by an information system.

Test Data   Data used only in a non-production mode to exercise and evaluate the operation of systems or application software.

Threat / Vulnerability Analysis   That element of the overall risk management process that deals with the identification and analysis of risk-causing weaknesses in security and the man-made or natural threats that exploit these weaknesses.

TIFF   (Tagged Image File Format) Standard graphics format developed by Aldus for the storage of high-resolution (greater than 72 dpi) scanned images that can be imported into a page-layout program.

Time Sharing Option   TSO - An integral component of the MVS operating system allowing interactive processing.

Token   A data packet used to transmit information on a token ring network.

Topology	The physical layout of network components (cable, stations, gateways, hubs, and so on). There are three basic interconnection topologies: star, ring, and bus network. On a star network, workstations connect directly to a file server but not to each other. On a ring network, the file server and workstations are cabled in a ring, and a workstation's messages may have to pass through several other workstations before reaching the file server. On a bus network, all workstations and the file server are connected to a central cable (called a trunk or bus).
Tracks	Physical locations on a data storage medium. On a disk, tracks take the form of concentric circles. Tracks are divided into sectors to form the fundamental units of disk storage.
Training	Personnel are provided explicit instructions and tested for their understanding before being assigned new duties.
Transactions	Application control statements which cause specific functions to be initiated, and which may be considered as privileged according to their functions.
Transmit	To send electronic signals from station to station through a communication medium (coaxial cable, twisted-pair cable, fiber optics, microwave, etc.).
Transmission Control Protocol	Transmission Control Protocol (TCP) and Internet Protocol (IP) was developed in 1974 by DARPA as part of the initial project efforts.
Trustee	A user who has been given specific rights to work in a particular network directory or sub-directory.
Trustee Rights	The rights granted to an individual user allowing that user to work in a particular directory or sub-directory. See also Rights.
TSO	Time Sharing Option
TSR	Abbreviation for "Terminate, Stay Resident." Synonym - "Memory Resident"
Typo	Short for typographical error.

Unauthorized Denial Of Service	An individual, either intentionally or unintentionally, abuses or misuses the network, rendering it useless or significantly disrupted. Examples of this are inserting operating system transactions to modify the network configuration, or overloading the network with a high volume of unauthorized transactions.
Unauthorized Insertion Of Information	An individual taps into a communication link and, using information about the system and TC/IP protocols (possibly via interception), pretends to be an authorized user in order to gain access to and insert transactions to manipulate enterprise information.
Unauthorized Interception	An individual taps into a communication link or a radio wave transmission to gain access to sensitive information, procedures, protocols, identification numbers and passwords.
Unauthorized Intrusion	An individual accesses a host or network without proper authorization for purposes of information browsing, analysis, disruption, damage, or fraud.
Uninterruptible Power Supply	UPS
Updating	Changing information in a file through the addition or subtraction from a value in a field.
Uploading	Sending data from your computer to another computer.
UPS	(Uninterruptible Power Supply) A generator that provides back-up power for a computer system. A UPS provides power for a short time; it's usually long enough for the original power source to be restored or the system to be safely shut down.
User	Any person accessing a PC, file server, mini-computer, mainframe computer system, computer data, or requesting processing services.
User Group	Organization in which computer users exchange tips and information.
User Interface	System by which information is exchanged between the user and the computer. Graphical interfaces such as the Macintosh and Microsoft Windows are best suited to desktop publishing.
Utility Program	A standard routine that performs a process required frequently such as sorting, merging, data transcription, printing, etc.

Value Analysis	That element of the overall risk management process that deals with the assignment of sensitivity of criticality ratings to major client server resources. Usually oriented towards specific applications, their associated data bases, equipment and the enterprise business functions which they support.
VGA	Display screen technology that provides 640 x 480 dots on the screen.
Violation	A security violation of access controls results when the authorization mechanism refuses to authorize an activity at some security checkpoint, such as logon, job initiation or file access attempt.
Violation Logging	Any system activity which fails authorization verification should cause a posting to a violations reporting log.
Volume	A portion of hard disk storage space of predetermined size. A volume is the highest level in a hierarchical directory structure (the same level as a DOS root directory). A hard disk is divided into one or more volumes by the network installer; these volumes can be divided into directories by network users who have the necessary rights.
Wait State	The period of time in which the computer "marks time" waiting for an operation to execute. For example, a wait state occurs when the faster CPU has to wait for information from an area of memory that doesn't execute as quickly.
WAN	(Wide-Area Network) A wide-area network spans greater distances than a LAN; WANs can span states or even continents.
Warm Boot	To reload a computer's operating system into memory while the computer is on. Warm boot an IBM PC-compatible computer by simultaneously pressing and holding the CTRL, ALT, and DEL keys. Then release them all. See also Boot.
Webpress	A press which prints on rolls (or 'webs') of paper (as opposed to a sheet feed press, which prints on cut sheets).
Widow	A single word or part of a word that appears as the last line of a paragraph.
Wild card Character	A special character recognized by a software application as a universal replacement for other characters. Two special characters ? and * can be used within a filename and its extension. These special characters give you greater flexibility with the DOS commands. For example, to copy all files in a directory with filenames that include the extension .COM, you would type COPY *.COM. The asterisk would represent any combination of characters that precedes the period.
Workstation	Any individual PC that is connected to a network (a network node) and is used to perform tasks (such as word processing) through the use of application programs or utilities.

Workstation Number	See Connection Number.
World Wide Web	Also known as WWW. Is a graphical interface to the Internet.
Worm	(Write-Once-Read-Many) A type of optical drive that allows you to write to the disk until the disk is full; at that point the disk becomes read-only. Information you have written to a WORM disk cannot be changed or erased. WORM drives are a good choice when a permanent audit trail is desired.
Wrap	Text contoured around illustrations of photos. Costly and time consuming to do without special machine capabilities.
Write	To record information on a hard disk, floppy diskette, or some other permanent storage device.
Write Protect	To prevent the data on one's disk from being altered.
WYSIWYG	(Pronounced wizzywig) What you see is what you get, i.e., the image on a computer monitor is an accurate representation of what will appear on a printed document. Many users prefer the term WYSIWMP (pronounced wizzywump: What you see is what might print).
WWW	See World Wide WEB
X-Height	The height of a lowercase letter excluding its ascenders and descenders.
Zero Wait State	The mode of computer operation that generally speeds processing by eliminating intentional pauses or waits.

Other PSR Offering

Client Server Management HandiGuide

MICROSOFT₅
WINDOWS™
COMPATIBLE

10 Reasons to use PSR's Client Server Management HandiGuide®

✔ Save your company hundreds of hours developing management and operating guidelines from scratch.

✔ Standardize the way Client Server is used and managed throughout your organization.

✔ Improve Client Server security procedures.

✔ Raise understanding of Client Server operations and management.

✔ Protect your enterprise's critical assets.

✔ Generate a Disaster Recovery Plan.

✔ Improve operator efficiency & reduce errors as general enterprise users gain a better understanding of their system.

✔ Create a back-up schedule using the guidelines and forms contained in the HandiGuide®.

✔ Use the tables and charts provided to define a more efficient operating environment.

✔ Use the HandiGuide® to design and structure the Client Server facilities, hardware, software and data in a way that has already been used and tested by many major enterprises.

Managing Client Servers -- The Challenge That Can Not Wait

There are three types of Client Server Managers and Users: those who have already failed in the eyes of the enterprise, those who are going to, and those who have prepared themselves and their enterprises with the right management tools to get the job done.

Client Server Management HandiGuide® contains over 325 pages of tools and practical tips for the non-technical manager and user as well as the technoligist. There are over 31 tables and charts that are used as guidelines and directives by some of the most successful enterprises in the world. Included are:

- *Sample organizational charts*
- *Responsibility matrix*
- *Functional and individual role definitions*
- *Sample work plans for risk assessment and application development*
- *Proven risk classification communication format*
- *Job description for Client Server system administrator*
- *Personal practices supporting hiring, training and all types of terminations*
- *Facilities requirements -- including management's needs from fire protection to security*
- *Asset protection and security requirements*

- *Insurance requirements definition*
- *Definition of components of a business resumption program*
- *LAN security including director and trustee rights definition*
- *Back-up and recovery guidelines and management tools including frequency and storage guidelines*
- *Audit trail definition*
- *System development life cycle for the Client Server and mainframe environment*
- *Documentation standards*
- *Service request (change management) process flow and data definitions*
- *Access control - physical, application*

Available Formats

Bound Book

Word processing files (comes with a bound book)
> Word for Windows 6.0 and up
> WordPerfect 5.2 and up

Electronic Book (comes with a bound book)
> Fully indexed network ready
> unlimited users requires Windows 95 or
> Windows NT annotations & book marks
> full Windows cut & paste

Conversions

PSR will convert your company policies and procedures or any other operations manual into an on-line electronic book. The electronic format is feature-rich, quick, and easy-to-use. Furthermore, it can be installed on a LAN for multiple users or a laptop for a field operator. Call for a quote.

PC
Policies and Procedures
Management HandiGuide®

Chapters Include

- Security Guidelines
- Local Area Networks
- Backup and Recovery
- Business Resumption Plan
- Applications Development Standards
- Internet
- Justification, Acquisition & Support
- Manager's Responsibilities
- Change Control
- How to get Technical Support

10 Reasons to use PSR's PC Policies and Procedures HandiGuide®

1. Save your company hundreds of hours developing PC policies and procedures from scratch.

2. Standardize policies and procedures throughout your organization.

3. Improve PC security procedures.

4. Raise understanding of PCs, LANs, and workstations with the aid of tables, illustrations, a comprehensive index, and a glossary of terms.

5. Protect your company from software copyright violations.

6. Generate a Disaster Recovery Plan.

7. Improve operator efficiency & reduce errors as general corporate users gain a better understanding of their system.

8. Create a backup schedule using the guidelines and forms contained in the HandiGuide®.

9. Use the guidelines and forms to control the acquisition of hardware and software, and save your company money.

10. Feel comfortable with the HandiGuide® since it has already been used and tested by major companies.

http://www.psrinc.com/policy.htm

Available Formats

- **Bound Book**

- **Word processing files**

  Word for Windows 6.0 and up
  or WordPerfect 5.2 and up

  comes with a bound book

- **Electronic Book**

  fully indexed
  network ready
  unlimited users
  requires 1 MB
  annotations & book marks
  full Windows cut & paste

  comes with bound book

MICROSOFT®
WINDOWS™
COMPATIBLE

Conversions

PSR will convert your company policies and procedures or any other operations manual into an on-line electronic book. The electronic format is feature-rich, quick, and easy-to-use. Furthermore, it can be installed on a LAN for multiple users or a laptop for a field operator.

Call for a quote.

Partial Client List

Intel Corporation	HBO & Company
E & J Gallo Winery	American Mutual Life
Twentieth Century Fox	University of Alabama
Keebler Company	Bergen Brunswig
Unitek/3M	Corporation
PacTel Cellular	Kraft General Foods
Carl Karcher Enterprises	Cardone Industries
Volvo North America	Random House, Inc.
City of Ann Arbor	Mazda Motor of America
Navel Education & Training	Inc.
The Gap Stores, Inc.	Day Runner, Inc.
Denny's	UCSF Medical Center
Coca-Cola Bottling	City of Palo Alto
DMV	Manufacturer's Hanover
Bose Corporation	Kiwi Brands, Inc.
Executone	Prudential
Bristol-Meyers Squibb Co.	Confederated Tribes
MGM/UA	A.T. Kearney Inc.
American Caner Society	First Interstate Bank
Beech Aircraft Corporation	Micron Technology
Land O' Lakes Inc.	Lackland Air Force Base
Reader's Digest	Dunkin' Donuts
CBS, Incorporated	Cablevision Systems
Interactive Business	Alabama River Pulp
Budget Rent-A-Car	Federal Reserve Bank
SmithKline Beecham	Shering-Plough Health
Ciba-Geigy Corporation	Care
Levi Strauss & Co.	International Technology
Cincinnati Gas and Electric	City Colleges of Chicago
Port Authority of NY & NJ	Griffen Hospital
Sony Corporation	DEP Corporation
FAA	PacifiCare
Ziff-Davis Publishing	Samsonite Corporation
Blue Cross/Blue Shield	L.A. Sheriff's Department
Astra Pharmaceutical	Anderson Consulting
Sizzler International, Inc.	Howard University
Home Savings of America	Southern California Edison
Turtle Wax, Inc.	Olin Corporation
Mitsubishi Electronics	Joseph E. Seagram & Sons
Lockheed Missiles & Space	California State University
Children's Hospital of LA	Pioneer-Standard
American Red Cross	Electronics
VISA U.S.A. Inc.	Stanford Telecomm.
United Way	Fireman's Fund Insurance
Ingram Micro	City of Milwaukee
MCA	Rush Prudential
DOT	Midcon Corporation
American Honda	Ashland Oil, Inc.
Allergan, Inc.	Health & Welfare
Merrill Lynch	Dakota County
Detroit Edison	Sandoz Chemicals
US Patent & Trademark	Mercy Hospital
Time Warner Inc.	Syracuse University
City of Cleveland	Rotary International
MW Kellogg Company	ITT Automotive
Dreyfus	Royal Bank of Trinidad
Caesars World	LA Gear
Sunbeam Oster	World Savings & Loan
Bureau of Land	Olympus America, Inc.
Capitol-EMI Music, Inc.	Mutual of Omaha
International City	Companies
Datamation	Reliance Electric Company
Target	New YorkCity Transit
Knapp Communications	Herman's Sporting Goods
General Electric	Loyola University
Playtex Apparel, Inc.	

Metrics HandiGuide ®

for the Internet and Information Technology

Topics Include

Internet, Electronic Communication, & LANS
Electronic Communication Usage Guidelines
    Electronic Mail
    Bulletin Boards

Metric Design
Reporting Audiences
    Reporting Levels
Report Groupings
    Financial
    Staffing
    Internet - Electronic Infrastructure

Metrics
    Report Categories
    Graphic Data Presentation
    Data Presentation Rules

Metric Implementation
    Metrics Management Loop
    IT Report Package
    SLA Report Package

Data Capture
    What is User Vision of Performance
    Monitors

Metrics System
    Select Metrics
    Capture and Record Data for Current Period
    View Documents

Sample Reports
    Financial
    Staffing
    Internet-electronic Infrastructure

Partial Client List

Capitol-EMI Music, Inc.
Harvard Community Health Plan
Nestle Food Company
Time Warner Inc.
Home Savings of America
Bristol-Meyers Squibb Company
People's Natural Gas
ITT Hartford Insurance Group
Northrop Corporation
Howard University
Kraft General Foods, Inc.
Dunkin' Donuts Inc.
William Wrigley Jr. Company
Federal Reserve Bank
Molson Breweries
Volvo-Data North America
LA Gear
Ingram-Micro, Inc.
Xerox Corporation
Polaroid Corporation
Los Angeles County
DEP Corporation
Hunt-Wesson Foods, Inc.
Computerworld
GMF Robotics
Southern California Edison
MGM/UA Communications Co.
General Electric Nuclear Energy
Micron Technology
Sadoz Chemicals
JC Penny Company, Inc.
Koch Industries
Samsonite Corporation
USAir, Inc.
City of Palo Alto
Metropolitan Life Insurance
Bank of California
WordPerfect Corporation
ARCO
Solvay Pharmaceutical
Rush Prudential Health Plans
Port Authority of NY & NJ
Southwestern Bell
American Airlines
Rotary International
City of Milwaukee
Reader's Digest
Collins Foods International
Borland International
Syracuse University
Paramount Communications
American Honda Motor Co.

http://www.psrinc.com/metrics.htm

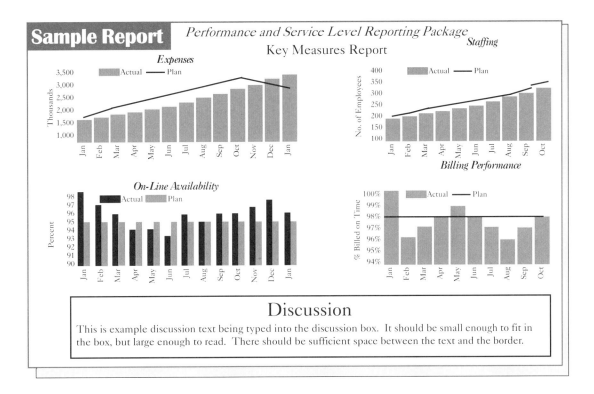

Available Formats

Bound Book

    With all report templates

Word Processing Format (comes with a bound book)

    Word for Windows 6.0 and up
    WordPerfect 5.2 and up

Electronic Book (comes with a bound book)

    Fully indexed network ready
    unlimited users requires Windows 95 or
    Windows NT annotations & book marks
    full Windows cut & paste

Metric System (comes with a bound book)

    Create your own metric reports using templates
    Change Discussion text with each report
    Update any number of reports during a session

MICROSOFT®
WINDOWS™
COMPATIBLE

Information Systems
Position Descriptions HandiGuide ®

Executives (level 1)

Chief Information Officer
Vice Presidents
Consulting Services
Administration
Information Systems
Human Resources
Technical Services

Senior Management (level 2)

Production Services
Systems & Programming
IS Planning
Technical Services
Systems
Data Processing

Middle Management (level 3)

Store Systems	Point of Sale Support	Technical Services
Information Systems	Office Automation	Training Documentation
Database	Applications	Communications
Production Services	Systems	Computer Operations
Systems & Programming	Capacity Management	Network Services
Production Support	Transaction Processing	Information Center

Staff (level 4)

Network Technician	Change Control Analyst
Senior Programmer	Data Security Administrator
4th GL Specialist	Forms & Graphics Designer
IS Planning Analyst	Junior Computer Operator
Production Control Analyst	Tape Librarian
Coordinator - POS	Disaster Recovery

http://www.psrinc.com/job.htm

Description Topics

- **Job Title**
  - Position Purpose
  - Problems and Challenges

- **Essential Position Functions**
  - Principal Accountabilities
  - Authority
  - Job Contacts
  - Job Specifications

- **Career Ladder**

- **SampleOrganization Charts**

- **Mandated Compliance**
  - All descriptions comply with ADA and Federal Laborr Standards.

Available Formats

- **Bound Book**
  Over 450 pages
  over 128 descriptions

- **Word processing files**
  Word for Windows 6.0 and up
  or WordPerfect 5.2 and up
  Comes with bound book

- **Electronic Book**
  Fully indexed
  Network ready
  Unlimited users
  Full Windows cut & paste
  Comes with bound book

MICROSOFT®
WINDOWS™
COMPATIBLE

Clients Include

The Gap Stores, Inc.	LA Gear
America West Airlines	USAir, Inc.
DePaul University	Schering-Plough Corporation
Time Warner Inc.	Goodyear Tire & Rubber
American Cancer Society	First Interstate Bank
Duracell, Inc.	Volvo North America
Anderson Consulting	State of Ohio
FAA	Playtex Apparel, Inc.
Brock Candy Company	Keebler Company
Mitsubishi Electronics	Lear Astronics
Countrywide Funding	Mattel Toys
DEP Corporation	University of Alabama
Detroit Edison	John Hancock Mutual
Armor All Products Corp.	Blue Cross/Blue Shield
Deloitte Touche	Caltrans
Paramount Communications	Southern Cal Edison
Minolta Corporation	Rush Prudential Health
Texas Instruments	REG
GMAC Mortgage Corporation	Micron Technology
Astra Pharmaceutical Products	General Electric
Technicolor, Inc.	Hunt-Wesson Foods
Dunkin' Donuts	Carl Karcher
PacTel Cellular	Knowledgeware, Inc.
US Army Corps of Engineers	United Way
Koch Industries	Port Authority of NY & NJ
Turtle Wax, Inc.	San Francisco
Kaiser Permanente	A.T. Kearney Inc.
Encyclopedia Briitannica, Inc.	American Savings and Loan
Capitol-EMI Music, Inc.	Ingram Micro, Inc.
Nissan Motor Corporation	Loyola University
Levi Strauss & Co.	Public Works Canada
Home Savings of America	MCA
Sony Manufacturing Co.	Goody Products Inc.
Girl Scouts of the USA	Rotary International
Whirlpool Financial Corporation	Bio Rad Laboratories
McDonnell Douglas	National Council/
Atmos Energy Corporation	Compensation Insurance
City of Minneapolis	Memorial Sloan-Kettering
Northrop Corporation	Howard University
SC Johnson Wax	JC Penny Company, Inc.
Oakland Unified School Dist.	Samsonite Corporation
Federal Reserve Bank	Maxicare Health Plans
HBO & Company	Syracuse University
Temple University	US Navy
William Wrigley Jr. Company	Confederated Tribes
Pioneer Standard	Sandoz Chemicals
Westinghouse Savannah Corp.	McKesson Corp.
Miami Herald Publishing Co.	
Collins Foods International	
Joseph E. Seagram & Sons	
Columbia Presbyterian Medical	

- Provides formal definition of the IS Organization
- Improves internal coordination
- Facilitates staff planning, organizational development, & resource acquisition
- Improves communications with other business functions resulting in better IS service levels
- Enhances effectiveness of IS recruiting programs

HandiGuide® Order Form

Item Description		Unit Price	Qty	Extended Price
Bound Books	❑ IS Position Description	$395.00		
	❑ PC Policies and Procedures	$395.00		
	❑ Internet and IT Metrics	$395.00		
	❑ Client Server Managment	$395.00		
	❑ Management Series (Set of all 4)	$1,195.00		
Word Processing Format[1,3] Circle format - Word for Windows, WordPerfect	❑ IS Position Description[5]	$795.00		
	❑ PC Policies and Procedures[5]	$795.00		
	❑ Client Server Management[5]	$795.00		
Metric System[3]	❑ Internet and IT Metrics[4,5]	$795.00		
Multi-Media Format[2]	❑ IS Position Description[3,5]	$895.00		
	❑ PC Policies and Procedures[3,5]	$895.00		
	❑ Client Server Management[3,5]	$895.00		
	❑ Internet and IT Metrics[3,5]	$895.00		
HandiGuide® Set [includes Book, Word Processing/System files and Multimedia]	❑ IS Position Description[5]	$995.00		
	❑ PC Policies and Procedures[5]	$995.00		
	❑ Client Server Management[5]	$995.00		
	❑ Internet and IT Metrics[5]	$995.00		
Bi-Monthly Newsletter	❑ Annual Subscription PSR Reviews	$59.95		
PSR Services	❑ Annual Salary Survey	$199.00		
	❑ Competitive Metrics	Call PSR		
	❑ Update Service	15%		

Payment Method:
(Payment in U.S. Dollars only)
- ❑ Mastercard
- ❑ Visa
- ❑ American Express
- ❑ Purchase Order
  (Domestic Orders Only)
- ❑ Check
- ❑ Wire Transfer (Call PSR)

California residents add applicable sales tax _____

Domestic Shipping & Handling (16.50 or Next Day at $24.00) _____

Total Order Amount: [6,7,8]

Credit Card No: ☐☐☐☐☐☐☐☐☐☐☐☐☐☐☐☐☐☐☐

Name on Credit Card: _____

Exp. Date: ☐☐ – ☐☐

Federal ID#: 95-3729780

Signature: _____
(Required for all orders)

Ship To

Name: _____

Company: _____

Street Address: _____

(No P.O. Box No.) _____

City, State, Zip: _____

Phone: _____ Fax: _____

Notes, terms, and conditions:

1. PC-compatible 3.5" media
2. Fully-indexed, run-time Multi-Media version compatible with Microsoft Windows 3.1, Windows 95 and NT.
3. One bound copy of HandiGuide® included
4. Requires proper 32 bit version of Microsoft 95 or NT plus Word for Windows
5. Annual Update Service available at 15% cost of item
6. All invoices are Net 10 days; late charges of 1.5% per month apply to all past due balances
7. All returns must be in perfect condition and require a return material authorization (RMA) number. A 25% restocking fee applies to all returns.
8. Payment in full or an approved company purchase order for the Total Order Amount must be attached to this order form

Positive Support Review, Inc. - (310) 453-6100 Fax: (310) 453-6253
2500 Broadway, Suite 320, Santa Monica, California 90404-3061

http://www.psrinc.com/psr.htm

Index

D